Beyond Baskets and Beads
Activities for Older Adults
With Functional Impairments

Beyond Baskets and Beads
Activities for Older Adults
With Functional Impairments

Mary Hart

Karen Primm

Kathy Cranisky

Venture Publishing, Inc.
State College, Pennsylvania

Production Manager: Richard Yocum
Manuscript Editing: Valerie Paukovits, Michele L. Barbin
Cover: Echelon Design
Artwork: David Porter

Library of Congress Catalogue Card Number 2003101953
ISBN 1-892132-42-7

Table of Contents

Acknowledgments

We gratefully acknowledge Dr. Karen Wolk Feinstein and Nancy Zionts from the Jewish Healthcare Foundation of Pittsburgh, PA, for funding the project and for their kindness and concern for the older population. We would also like to acknowledge our contributing agencies: Council Care Adult Services, The Jewish Community Center, and Vintage (all of Pittsburgh, PA) as well as Presbyterian SeniorCare, Woodside Place (of Oakmont, PA). Special thanks to Rita Smiddle, Leslie Swiantek, Jamie Typovksy, and Leslie Wright, principal contributors to this book. Thanks, too, to our illustrator, Dave Porter, for knowing exactly what we were looking for even when we didn't know. Finally, we thank California University of Pennsylvania, whose commitment to community service allows the Center in the Woods to continue to serve older adults throughout our region. *Beyond Baskets and Beads: Activities for Older Adults With Functional Impairments* is dedicated to older adults who despite functional impairments inspire us with their indomitable strength and their ability to get on with the business of living.

Preface

For many of you, the word "manual" may conjure up visions of a boring, preachy text, which after a cursory look winds up on a bookshelf collecting dust. We tried calling our book something else, but "guidebooks" are for tourists, "directories" belong to the phone company, and no one was quite sure who would want a "compendium." So the bad news is—we admit it—this is a manual.

Now for the good news—you don't have to bother clearing a space on your shelf for it. Why? Because this is a reference you will want to keep close at hand to refer to on a regular basis. In other words, this is the manual you will actually use! Are we tooting our own horn? Darn right, we are. Do we believe what we're saying? We really do.

This project was born out of love. An officer of the Jewish Healthcare Foundation visited adult day centers looking for a program for her husband's mother. She found participants being asked to color with crayons like pre-schoolers and to take part in other inappropriate activities. The daughter-in-law was horrified. Despite functional impairments due to Alzheimer's disease, her mother-in-law, a woman of culture and style, deserved better. The Jewish Healthcare Foundation officer set out to develop a manual of culturally appropriate and age-appropriate activities for older adults with functional impairments.

Our facility, the Center in the Woods, located in California, Pennsylvania, was fortunate enough to be chosen to develop this manual. The Center in the Woods is a gerontological center serving individuals 60 and over. Our mission is to improve the quality of life for older adults in Southwestern Pennsylvania. To serve older adults with functional impairments, our facility includes an adult day center, which provides a stimulating, safe, and structured environment for physically and mentally impaired older adults.

We don't claim to have a magic formula. Our tips and guidelines were developed through trial and error with generous amounts of brainstorming, foot stomping, and teeth gnashing thrown in. When something didn't work, we went back to the drawing board again and again. This book contains all the things we wish someone had told us when we started. We hope that our experiences will help you to avoid some pitfalls and false starts, and ultimately to provide the best participant-centered activities for the older adults in your program.

Chapter 1
No Hand Turkeys, Please:
Philosophical Issues That Impact a Successful Program

When we visited an adult day center at Thanksgiving, we found the participants tracing their hands on paper to make turkey drawings—an activity that
most second graders would find beneath their dignity. To be blunt, *we had a cow
over those turkeys.* One staff member's reaction was, "When I'm in a nursing
home, you won't make me do hand turkeys, will you?" She was joking—but
not entirely.

   On the following pages we've outlined a few of the elements that we
consider to be essential to any successful program. Some relate to the activities
themselves and others to the staff's approach, but all are critical.

   We often hear someone say, "You know how old people are." Yes, we do.
They are happy and sad, fascinating and boring, polite and rude, caring and
inconsiderate. They run the gamut of traits and emotions just like all human
beings. There is a popular myth that all older people share similar personalities
and abilities. Nothing could be further from the truth. The only thing they share
is that they have lived a certain number of years on earth. Yet, we don't explain
behaviors by saying, "you know how 30-year-olds are" or "middle-aged people
do that." If anything, older people are more different because they have lived

longer and experienced more. By denying older adults their individuality, we rob them of their most precious possessions—their unique identities.

We have found that the most basic traits remain intact long after some memory loss and confusion have surfaced. For example, one of our staff was sitting with an adult day participant in our dining room. The staff member was trying to coax Esther, an 80-year-old woman with Alzheimer's disease, to eat lunch. While unable to communicate her reason, Esther steadfastly refused to begin. Our staff member finally realized that Esther's reluctance had nothing to do with a lack of appetite. She had been raised to wait until everyone at the table was served before beginning to eat. Her upbringing would not allow her to eat before her dining companions. Esther's memory may be failing, but her manners are not.

In recognition of the vast differences among your participants, activity choices are critical. A former executive who never had an interest in crafts does not necessarily want to learn to make a potpourri basket at this point in life— or maybe he or she does. To the greatest degree possible, the choice should belong to the person. This means offering a wide variety of activity choices and individualizing your program to meet the diverse needs of your population.

Appropriateness

A facility for adults should never resemble a preschool class. While activities should take into consideration the participants' physical and mental capabilities, they should never be childish or demeaning.

When in doubt, ask yourself, "Would I be insulted to be asked to take part in this activity?" We don't mean to imply that all activities must be serious. One of our favorite activities is balloon volleyball. Sure it works toward a number of goals—motor, social, and so on—but its main therapeutic value is that it's a lot of fun. Toss a balloon into a group of adults at a picnic or other recreational setting, and you'll most likely set off an impromptu round of volleyball. It's enjoyable, and almost everyone can participate. If you compare this to the reaction that crayons and coloring books would evoke from a similar group—especially if they were pressured to take part—you'll understand how we decide on appropriateness.

The diversity of your population will also help to determine which activities are appropriate for your facility. The popularity of doll collecting in this country demonstrates that toys are not just for children. If you have a participant comforted by having a doll, whether it reminds her of a hobby or of her years as a mother, we feel that it would be appropriate to let her have one. On the other hand, this does not mean that you should randomly hand out dolls to all of your participants. Some will almost certainly be insulted. The key is to know the people you work with and to plan your activities accordingly.

Cultural and Ethnic Variety

Do culture and ethnicity play a part in your center? Before you say "no," stop to think. Do you serve corned beef and cabbage on St. Patrick's Day? Do you play polkas on the radio because some of your people enjoy them? Do you decorate for Christmas, Hanukkah, or other holidays? If so, you've already begun to incorporate cultural and ethnic themes into your center.

Culture, by one definition, reflects "the concepts, habits, skills, art...of a given people in a given period." Ethnicity is "group consciousness based on a sense of common origins." The ways in which culture and ethnicity influence your program will depend on the makeup of your population.

In some cases, the cultural variations may not be great. Many of your participants may have been born or lived a large number of years in the United States during a similar span of time and share a great deal of history. If, on the other hand, many of your participants are relatively recent immigrants, the cultural differences may be more pronounced.

The degree to which ethnicity plays a part in your center will also vary. Most or all of your participants may be of similar ethnic background, or you may have a melting pot. Some participants will proudly share their ethnic heritage, while others feel far removed from their roots. By knowing your participants you will be able to include culturally and ethnically relevant activities in your program. Sometimes it's a simple matter of respect and recognition of your participants. If you are going to recognize the holidays of one religion, you cannot ignore those of another.

Allow your participants, volunteers, and staff members to take a turn at teaching about their backgrounds through discussion groups, theme days or meals, holiday celebrations, and so on. If you do not find enough diversity within your center, look for ways to reach into the community through religious congregations, minority action groups, and other resources. You can even stretch the definition of "culture" by learning about and observing the traditions of your participants' families and communities.

Sometimes, including such activities is just plain fun. Ethnic foods, whether in recognition of your participants or just for variety, can spice up your menus. Why not have a Cinco de Mayo celebration—even if you don't have a single person of Mexican descent among your group? Everyone can enjoy an extra fiesta—sometimes all the more for never having celebrated it before. You're never too old to try something new, and your participants aren't either.

Meaningfulness

Would you want to complete a puzzle only to have someone dump it out and say "do it again?" Or spend laborious hours stringing beads only to have a staff member unstring them at the end of the day? Of course not, and neither do your participants.

Puzzles and beads are both fine if the person enjoys these activities. Wouldn't it be better to offer a choice of a different puzzle when the first is completed? Why not use the completed string of beads as a prize or gift? Is it really worth conserving a few cents worth of beads at the price of someone's dignity and self-esteem?

Activities need to be meaningful. If your participants are going to cook a meal, make sure that they know what it is for—to be served at lunch, perhaps, or delivered to a homebound person. Gardeners can derive satisfaction when they see the flowers they helped to care for gracing your center, or the produce they cultivated finding its way onto the table.

When a craft is completed, the crafter should be able to feel proud of his or her efforts and to see a use for the end result. In planning a project, be sure to consider the functional level of the participants. Modifications need to be made so that they can feel proud of, rather than embarrassed by, their end result.

It's a fact of life—the older we get, the less time we have left, making each hour even more precious. Your participants should feel that their time is valuable. They deserve to fill their days with enjoyable and fulfilling activities.

Autonomy

Choices—our lives are filled with them. From what to eat for breakfast to how we earn our living, having choices is a part of being alive. We begin offering choices to our children at the youngest possible age. "Do you want to wear the striped shirt or the plain one?" "Would you like a peach or a pear?" We recognize that decision making is a necessary life skill and a critical factor in the formation of self-esteem.

For most people, some choices are taken away as they age. Careers are over, children have been raised, and physical health limits activities. However, our need for autonomy—the right of an individual to govern himself or herself according to his or her own reason—remains. It is possible to arrange your facility to offer many choices. In which activities do people choose to participate? Will they eat with the group or do they prefer their own company? Participants have the right to make choices whenever possible.

In the case of people with significant impairments, you may be tempted to make all of the decisions for them. Try to resist! Even if you doubt whether you will be understood, offer a choice whenever you can. This will show respect for your participants and may sometimes elicit an unexpected and welcome response.

Health and safety issues must be considered, but sometimes these precautions are overemphasized to the detriment of self-esteem and autonomy. If we were to exercise the utmost caution, everyone would wear disposable gloves to knead bread dough. We would exclude participants from the kitchen to eliminate the possibility of a sneeze. No one but staff would be allowed near the stove or knives. *We don't choose to run our Center this way.*

We practice good hygiene, but can live with the risk of a stray germ. Sometimes people from outside our Center are surprised by our philosophy. "You let Martha handle a sharp knife? But she's so confused!" While it's true that Martha is often confused and forgetful, she is also perfectly capable of handling a knife, and we won't take that away from her. There may seem to be a fine line between "too careful" and "not careful enough," but it's one we feel comfortable walking.

Look for ways to allow people to use skills they have learned throughout their lives. A retired teacher has spent the better part of his life making decisions that affected the education of hundreds of students. Although he may no longer be able to plan a curriculum or write a lesson plan, he may be able to read a book to a child or lead a discussion group among fellow book lovers. He continues to do a job related to his life's work and can feel satisfaction in the contribution he continues to make.

Many of our programs are designed to fill the basic human need we all share—to feel useful. As Dr. Orbra C. Hulsey puts it, "People will be happy in about the same degree that they are helpful." Some of our participants can cook or help to bake cookies for our bake sales. Others harvest vegetables or build displays for our festivals. Some like to fold towels and other laundry. Most can help in some way, even if it takes some brainstorming on the part of the staff.

We can hear all of you activity directors saying, "What staff?" Good question. This is where volunteers can make or break your program. If you don't have the staff to offer individualized activities, you have to be creative about recruiting and using your volunteers (more about this in Chapter 3). We don't limit activities because of staff shortage—we find volunteers to help.

Respect and Preservation of Dignity

Every person has the right to be treated with respect. It is not enough that your staff help a participant to change after a bathroom accident—they must take the situation in stride, with assurances that this is "no big deal."

Imagine being on a shopping trip with a friend. As you browse through the racks, you begin to feel a little queasy. You start toward the restroom and realize, to your horror, that you are not going to make it. Instead, the remains of your breakfast make a return appearance all over your clothes, the floor, and everything else within striking distance. There is no way around it—this is an embarrassing experience. You would probably begin saying things like, "I can't imagine what came over me" and "This has never happened to me before."

Your friend could react in a number of ways. What if she showed her disgust in word or expression? Even worse, she could say things like, "Why didn't you get to the restroom sooner?" or "Look what a mess you've made of yourself!" What do you think this would do to your friendship?

On the other hand, imagine that your friend takes the whole situation in stride. She helps you get to the restroom, all the while making pleasant small talk. She calmly helps you clean up and goes to get fresh clothing for you. When you apologize and try to thank her, she says, "You'd do it for me, wouldn't you?" This is a friend you would trust with your life.

Working with people is not for the fainthearted. We humans are a messy business. We sneeze, cough, bleed, and do a host of other things to which we would rather not admit. A bathroom accident should not require any more apology than a sneeze or a hiccup—they're all bodily functions that a person may not be able to control at times.

Attitude is everything. This atmosphere of respect and preservation of dignity must pervade a facility. Nowhere is it more true that you must put yourself in the other person's shoes, and treat him or her as you would want to be treated.

Listening

Are you *listening* to me? We've probably all heard the question—and asked it, too. The truth is we're all guilty of listening with "half an ear"—hearing the sounds without processing the information. At home and on the job, with children, spouses, and co-workers, we hear without listening.

Hearing is a passive, automatic process. Because we can't close our ears, we hear sounds whether we want to or not. Listening, on the other hand, is a skill. It is an active process. It takes concentration. It takes work.

Listening is probably the most important part of communication. Are you a good listener? Try the quiz below. If you answer honestly, you probably won't get a perfect score.

1. Do you think of other things when someone is talking?

2. Do you doodle, look around the room, and fidget?

3. Do you argue silently with the person?

4. Do you think about what you will say next?

5. Do you listen without facial expression?

6. Do you frequently interrupt?

7. Do you try to finish a speaker's sentence?

8. Do you pay more attention to how something is said (e.g., grammar, voice, choice of words) than to the content?

All "No" answers mean that you are a world-class listener. "Yes" answers indicate areas for improvement. Target one, and start listening. People may have a lot more to say than you think.

Kindness

Webster's defines kindness as the state of being "sympathetic, friendly, gentle, tenderhearted, generous." Whether it shows itself as a genuine smile, a pat on the back, or a sincere interest in another person, most of us can recognize kindness when we see it.

It may be harder to put kindness into practice, however. It's often too easy to get caught up in the pressures of the day. When your desk is buried in paperwork, it's tempting to brush off the older person who "just wants to talk" so that you can get back to work. Guess what? We believe that stopping to talk to a participant who needs you *is* your work. That paperwork doesn't care whether it gets done today or not, but you could miss a golden opportunity to make a difference for a fellow human being.

Being kind does not mean being patronizing. Just because a person has reached the senior years does not mean he or she wants to be called "Honey" or "Sweetie." Remember that the Pope and the Chief Justice are both senior citizens. Your participants deserve the same measure of respect. Save the endearments for your significant other or your cat.

Kindness seems to come more naturally to some people than to others. Can you teach kindness? We think you can. Our Center runs kindness workshops for staff and volunteers. We stress the importance of maintaining a positive attitude. We emphasize how important a smile or a greeting can be. We teach skills to turn a negative situation into a positive one. The image of our Center depends on each and every one of our staff members, volunteers included, and we make sure that they understand that. These staff members and volunteers then become role models for others. We conclude this chapter with a popular story that illustrates our concept of kindness:

As a young man walked the beach at dawn, he noticed an old man ahead of him picking up starfish and flinging them into the sea.

Catching up with the gentleman, he asked him why he was doing this. The old man answered that the stranded starfish would die if left until the morning sun.

"But the beach goes on for miles and there are millions of starfish!" countered the young man. "How can your efforts make a difference?"

The old man looked at the starfish in his hand, threw it safely into the waves, and replied, "It makes a difference to this one."

Chapter 2
A Circle of Friends:
The Participant-Centered Approach

Take a moment to think about the people in your care. Do you know what they did for a living? What about their children and grandchildren? Do you know what they like in their coffee, or if they prefer tea? If the answers are no, then your facility hasn't been using the participant-centered approach. We hope that we can convince you to change that.

This chapter is likely to elicit groans from busy activity directors. "But I have 20 (or 30 or 40) impaired elders in my care," you may say. "Who has the time?"

We empathize. The participant-centered approach can be time-consuming and labor-intensive. Yet we can't imagine running our facility any other way. Before you assume that we are a large and wealthy center with staff bursting from our seams, let us assure you that this is far from the case. Our participant focus is driven by our commitment, our staff's creativity, and a lot of wonderful volunteers. We treat people as individuals, not an amorphous group known as "the impaired elderly." We learn as much about each participant as we possibly can—his or her education, career background, hobbies, favorite music, and so on. Then we do our best to incorporate that information into designing our programs.

Most of us who work with the elderly are required to do a certain number of standardized assessments to meet licensing requirements. Instrumental activities of daily living… environmental assessments… activity observation scale…

leisure interest survey... the list goes on and on. Sometimes it seems that the day is fast approaching when there will be more assessment tools than there are people to assess!

We suspect that more often than not these assessments are performed, documented, and filed away until the next inspector comes along. They serve a limited purpose, but rarely make any impact on a participant's daily life. Why don't standardized tests work? Because they ignore the fact that we humans stubbornly refuse to be pigeonholed into "standards." We insist on being different, each one of us a unique and wonderful individual. We are a planet full of square pegs. Here is an example from our adult day center:

> *Gary, who has Alzheimer's disease, lived in a personal care home for over a year. His caregiver felt that he would also benefit from a program like our adult day center and enrolled him. When the staff did their initial assessment, Gary was unhappy and combative. However, when Gary began the program, the staff got to know him as a person and learned that he had a great love for big band music. Now we dance with Gary and listen to music with him. Although Gary is losing ground, he can still converse about musical instruments and composers. He is happy and energetic with us and exhibits none of the violent behavior seen during his "standardized" assessment. He also listens to "his" music at his personal care home. The personal care home staff was so amazed at the dramatic transformation they saw in Gary that they have asked to be trained by our adult day staff. More importantly, Gary now has joy in his life.*

If our staff had not been so attuned to Gary, they might never have found the key to reaching him. The adult day staff then shared their knowledge with everyone else in Gary's life—other staff members, volunteers, his caregiver, and the personal care staff. Now we all know how to reach Gary through his love of music.

Too often we only know people as they are today, failing to recognize that each person is the sum total of the experiences that make up his or her life. We believe that this is where many of the usual assessment tools fall short. Most of them are a checklist format—easy to complete, but almost impossible to recall or to use in any meaningful way. Most of the questions asked are also closed-ended, requiring only a brief response. They don't encourage the in-depth kind of conversation that can get at the personal and truly pertinent information. Many assessments also fail to take into account the information that can be gleaned from families and caregivers—those who really know the person in question. If the participant cannot express his or her feelings adequately, a loved one may help to fill the gaps.

On the next few pages we have reproduced our own assessment form, written as an outline to complete the life story of the participant. A volunteer interviews the caregiver(s) and the participant, if possible. When the form has been filled in as completely as possible, the results are bound into a short story with pictures supplied by the family. A family member is asked to read the completed story into an audio or video recorder. The book and tape then become a keepsake for the family. Interview results are used in planning programs. Watching a tape of a loved one reading his or her story can also be used to reassure a person who is restless or agitated. Now instead of a cold list of facts, we have a biography of a fascinating human being.

Each new staff person or volunteer who will work with a participant is required to read, listen to, or watch the story of the participant's life. Admittedly, this takes time, but it is time very well spent. The woman with Alzheimer's disease becomes someone's mother and grandmother, a lady who owned her own business or lived in Paris. The frail elderly man regains his status as the president of a company or a skilled surgeon or a onetime star of the gridiron. No longer is this person to be pitied or patronized. Instead, we see a person to be admired and respected—a person approaching the latter part of a full and useful lifetime.

Once we see the person as a whole, it is easier to remember that Mrs. Smith loved to garden and might want to help with the planting. The staff and volunteers enjoy their introduction to our participants through their life stories. They remember more about each person and can use this knowledge in their interactions. The Life Story gives us a head start on getting to know our people and helps us to recognize the unique and special gifts each one brings to our Center.

The Life of

_____
(full name)

Childhood

_____ was born in _____
(first name)   (city, state, country)

in _____. There were _____ members in _____ family. They
(year)   (number)   (his/her)

included _____ mother, _____,
(first name)   (mother's full name)

father _____, and _____
(father's full name)   (siblings and pets)

_____

_____.

When _____ was a little _____, _____ lived
(first name)   (boy/girl)   (he/she)

in _____ in _____.
(house, apartment)   (town, state)

_____ was _____
(town)   (rural/urban)

_____.
(describe area)

When _____ was a
(first name)

little _____, _____
(boy/girl)   (he/she)

_____
(childhood information: friends, favorite toy, etc.)

_____

_____

_____

Photo From Childhood

_____ Completed _____ years of education. _____
(first name)   (number)   (he/she)

attended _____
(name of schools, field of interest, activities, etc.)

_____

_____

Early Adulthood

When _____ was
(first name)

_____ years old, _____ got _____
(age)   (he/she)   (his/her)

first job_____
(describe, including pay)

_____

Photo From Early Adulthood

_____.

_____ has spent most of _____ life _____
(first name)   (his/her)

_____
(describe career, life activities, church, clubs, etc.)

_____

_____

_____

Life With Partner

When _____ was _____ years old _____ met _____
(first name)   (age)   (he/she)   (his/her)

future partner, _____. _____
(partner's full name)   (partner's first name)

was _____
     (describe partner)

_____

_____

_____ and _____ had a ceremony
(first name)   (partner's first name)

_____
     (describe, date, place, etc.)

_____

_____ .

While _____ and
     (first name)

_____ were
(partner's first name)

Photo With Partner

together, they lived _____

_____
(describe location, house, etc.)

_____

_____ and _____ most memorable
(first name)   (partner's first name)

experience as a couple was _____

_____
(describe)

_____

_____

_____ was with _____ for
(first name)   (partner's first name)

_____ years. _____
(describe life with partner)

_____

_____

_____ is of _____
(first name)   (cultural background)

descent. Some of the cultural holidays

and events _____
(first name)

observed as a child included

_____
(describe holidays/traditions observed)

_____

_____   Photo From Holdiay/Special Event

_____

_____ partner is of _____
(first name)   (cultural background)

descent. _____
(partner's first name)   (describe life now)

_____

_____

_____

Of all _____ achievements_____ has been most proud of
(first name)   (he/she)

_____

_____

_____

_____

_____

Childrearing Years

When _____ was _____ years old _____
          (first name)   (age)   (he/she)

had/adopted _____ first child, a _____. _____ name is
                 (his/her)   (boy/girl)   (his/her)

_____.
  (child's name)

_____ was named
     (child's name)

after _____.

_____ had/adopted
    (first name)

more children. _____

_____

Photo of Children

_____

_____

_____
                    (list names and ages of children)

One of _____ most memorable experiences as a
              (first name)

_____ was _____
     (mother/father)   (describe)

_____

_____

Other significant individuals in _____ life include
(first name)

_____
(list and describe relationship)

_____

_____

_____ currently has _____ children still living,
(first name)   (number)

and _____ grandchildren.
(number)

_____
(list names, ages, where they live, etc.)

_____

_____

_____

_____

Photo of Grandchildren

A Typical Day in the Life of

_____

_____ normally gets up at _____. The first
(first name)   (time)

thing _____ does is _____
(he/she)   (describe)

_____

For breakfast _____ usually eats _____
(first name)   (describe meal)

_____

_____ .

_____ spends most of _____ day doing _____
(first name)   (his/her)

_____
(describe daily activities)

_____

_____ gets the most enjoyment out of _____ day when
(first name)   (his/her)

_____

_____

At around _____ , _____ starts to relax by
              (time)   (first name)

_____
(describe activities)

_____

_____

_____ usually turns the sheets down and settles into bed at
(first name)

_____ .
   (time)

Additional Notes

_____ now resides
(first name)

_____
(address, town, with whom, etc.)

_____

_____

Current Photo

Some of _____ favorite foods are _____
                (first name)   (list)

_____.

Some of _____ favorite activities include _____
                (first name)   (list)

_____.

The best times of _____ life were _____
                       (first name)   (describe)

_____

_____

Chapter 3
Meeting Them in the Parking Lot:
Getting and Keeping Volunteers

Volunteers! You love them—you hate them. You get them—you lose them. The bottom line is *you need them*. Unless your facility has unlimited funding, you just can't run a participant-centered program without lots of trained volunteers.

There are tons of good books on volunteers—and a few not so good ones. We don't claim to be experts. What we do say about volunteers is that "we get 'em, we train 'em, and we keep 'em." We have over 400 volunteers in our senior center and adult day program who are vital to our assessment process, our activities program, and almost every other aspect of our Center's success.

Getting 'Em

We get our volunteers from the same places you probably get yours—churches, social organizations, and so on. We also try sources like university students, fraternities and sororities looking for service projects, and high school students on breaks and summer vacations.

One difference in our approach to recruiting volunteers is that we take everything to the "nth" degree. Let's say we are approaching an area church. Do we call the pastor and ask for his help? Definitely, but we don't stop there. We offer to speak to the women's group, the men's group, the youth group, and any other group. We write a plea for the church bulletin or newsletter.

We might even attend a service or help with the spaghetti dinner so that we can speak to members personally. In a year or so, we may do the whole pitch all over again. We never let the community forget about the good work that we do, or that we can use their help.

A personal approach is key to finding good volunteers. We talk to everyone—community leaders, former caregivers, retirees, and so on. We also talk to people who donate to us. If they believe in us strongly enough to give donations, they may want to give their time, too, and see how their money is being used. Probably our best sources of volunteers are the families of our participants. Like our donors, they have a personal stake in our success.

Be Creative

One of our staff heard on the Saturday night newscast that a local fraternity had been cited for underage drinking. She knew that they would probably lose their charter and have to perform community service to regain it. Bright and early Sunday morning, she showed up at their door saying, "Hi! I'm from the Center in the Woods. I hear that you guys need a place to do some volunteer work." This woman has become such an expert at recruitment that we kid her about meeting potential volunteers in the parking lot. This same staff member also keeps a "hit list" of potential volunteers, including people nearing retirement.

It's important to have the right person do the asking. Someone who has a personal link to your potential volunteer, such as a friend, family member, or co-worker, is more likely to meet with success. Use your staff wisely in this respect, also. Choose the person whom everyone likes but no one can say "no" to. (Every organization has at least one of these.)

You need to be as specific as possible about the commitment you need from volunteers. Chances are you will get more than you ask for, and it will be given willingly. One of our volunteers was asked to fill in for our Meals on Wheels program when our regular driver was unavailable. He did it. He liked it. Ten years later, he's still delivering meals—and jokingly refers to himself as a "temporary volunteer."

We also take what we can get when it comes to a time commitment. A volunteer who can't spare two days a week might give one; another might help twice a month. A true example from our Center:

> *The staff in our adult day center accidentally set off our fire alarm, summoning the fire department. After the Fire Chief had determined that there was no real emergency, he got ready to leave but couldn't find his men. We located them in another part of the building—mov-*

ing a large screen television for our *"meet them in the parking lot"* staff member. It only took a few minutes but accomplished a job for us that needed to be done.

Combining a volunteer's skills and interests with the right job will lead to job satisfaction and high performance. In other words, you have to get to know your volunteers before you can help them find their niche. Learn about their background and experience, but also what they would enjoy doing.

When the mother of one of our directors began volunteering at our Center, we goofed. We knew that the woman was efficient and dependable and had a background in office work, so we assigned her to a variety of clerical tasks. She was very good at the work, but wasn't enjoying it. What she really wanted to do was to work with people—a task at which she also excels. We moved her to our health clinic where she can use her skills and she is much happier.

Training 'Em

Imagine yourself as a new volunteer at a nursing home. A harried-looking nurse at the front desk directs you to "Recreation" where an equally harried recreation director hands you a clipboard and tells you that you will be making "visits" today. "Start at the fifth floor and work down," she says. "Even if you just say 'hello,' make a record of it." You've just had your volunteer training.

After maneuvering your way to the fifth floor, you begin stopping at any open doorway to say "hello." There are few responses. You have no clue whether the people you "visit" can hear you, understand you, or even speak English. You dutifully note everything on the clipboard.

On the fourth floor, a woman sits alone in her room, crying softly. "My husband died," she explains between sobs. You murmur some appropriate phrases, pat her shoulder, and leave, feeling unprepared to cope with her grief. You decide that she is confused and obviously relives her husband's death daily. If her loss were recent, she wouldn't have been left alone, right? With relief, you note that your volunteer time is nearly up and head downstairs to turn in your clipboard.

As you get ready to leave, you think to ask about the woman in Room 420. "Oh, you mean Mrs. Smith? Yes, it's very sad. She shared that room with her husband, but he passed away this morning." You leave as quickly as possible, wondering whatever made you think that you wanted to volunteer.

Farfetched? Not at all. One of our staff had this experience when she volunteered for the first time at a nursing home/health-related facility in New York City in the 1970s. Could it happen today? We'd like to say no, but the truth is that very few agencies take the time to train their volunteers adequately.

No one would dream of putting a new employee to work with no orientation or training, yet this is routinely done with volunteers. Why? Perhaps you've experienced a parade of "revolving door" volunteers, and hesitate to invest time in someone who might not show up next time. However, this same lack of training and attention might be exactly the *reason* that your volunteers don't stay!

This may seem like a Catch-22 situation, but it really isn't. Except for the obvious benefit of a paycheck, volunteer workers are looking for the same payoffs as your other workers—job satisfaction, a feeling of making a difference, a chance to learn new skills, and an opportunity to grow.

We've found that volunteers who really feel that their work is important can be just as dedicated as our paid employees—sometimes even more so. While it's true that a volunteer can quit without notice or just plain not show up, so can an employee. It goes with the territory. When a volunteer is matched with an appropriate job, given the necessary training, and made to feel that he or she is making a difference, the chances are very good that you will gain a first-rate addition to your staff.

One of our loyal volunteers arrived at the Center one day obviously feeling under the weather. Someone asked why she didn't just go home. Our volunteer replied that if she were at work she probably *would* go home. She went on to explain that "I'm a volunteer, I don't have sick leave." Needless to say, she stayed on for the day.

What about that volunteer who just isn't working out? We've had this experience on a couple of occasions. First, see if you've got a good fit between the volunteer and the job. A bossy volunteer can be moved to a position where a take-charge approach is appropriate, or to one where he or she works solo. The volunteer who is not a self-starter can be paired with a supervisor who can offer the necessary direction. If you are willing to give the matter a little time and thought, you can probably find another job for most anyone.

In some cases, a volunteer will know that things are not working out and be uninterested in a different position. Accept a decision to "resign" with grace, thank him or her, and make leaving as painless as possible—just like you would for any other staff member.

Keeping 'Em

We'll do just about anything legal to keep a good volunteer. Following are some ideas that have worked for us.

- We hold regular meetings for our volunteers. These recognize their importance, give them a chance to make suggestions or bring up problems, and make them feel a part of the overall team.

- We hold luncheons, parties, and other special events in honor of our volunteers and recognize them with certificates or other small tokens that represent how we feel. We even invite their families to join us. We had a "Harry Day" for one of our most dedicated volunteers, a retired doctor who has come in at 7:45 a.m. every day for over ten years to do the tedious and time-consuming task of keeping records of our participants. We had a surprise breakfast, invited old and new friends, made him a "Gold Card Member," and had everyone write about Harry in a keepsake book. It took a little work, but not nearly as much as it would to try to replace Harry.

- We try to be—dare we say it—"volunteer-centered." We get to know our volunteers as friends, share stories about ourselves, and laugh—a lot. We need and care about our volunteers and aren't afraid to show it. At Christmas, three of our staff dressed up as elves and went door to door singing carols and spreading holiday cheer (we hope). We did our own Center in the Woods version of *The Night Before Christmas* and served lunch to one of our top volunteers.

- We send birthday and holiday cards with handwritten notes from staff members, and find other ways to recognize special occasions. We made one of our volunteers "Queen for a Day." We barged into a class she was taking with cake, crown (a fast-food giveaway which we spray-painted silver), flowers, and a "royal robe" (an expensive towel belonging to our director). When our "queen" left, waving and telling us how much she loved us, no one had the heart to mention that she was leaving with the towel. As our director said, "Towels are replaceable; good volunteers aren't."

- We submit photos and news releases to local papers on our volunteers. We love to see them get the recognition they deserve.

- We give as much credit as possible to our volunteers. Staff members have to be willing to take a back seat—what has been called a "passion for anonymity." We never forget our volunteers are working for personal satisfaction only, and we try to be sure that they find it. We remember that most people can live for a week on one good compliment.

- We listen to volunteer suggestions and ideas and give them the same consideration as if they came from a staff member.

- We train our volunteers initially, then offer opportunities for ongoing training. They are invited to in-service workshops, seminars, and other educational events.

- We treat our volunteers as staff members, include them in decision making, and ask their advice. They appear on our organizational chart. We encourage our staff to look on volunteers not as a nuisance or a threat, but as a valuable part of the staff who help to make our Center a better place.

Our volunteers show their love for our Center in many ways, both large and small. One chose the color scheme for our entire facility, while another asked us to buy a rubber mat to preserve the floor under the coffee pot. Our "wandering courtyard" in the adult day center was designed by a volunteer at a substantial savings over our original plans. An 80-year-old volunteer bought and planted two bushes to beautify our grounds. These contributions and so many others demonstrate the pride in ownership that our volunteers feel for our Center.

You get the idea. Volunteers are not a "frill" in our Center, but a fundamental part of the basic structure. We need and love and appreciate them—and we tell them so. We also remember that the best way to keep good people is to give them room to grow.

Chapter 4
Almost Home:
Adapting the Physical Environment

What does the word "home" mean to you? Comfort? Acceptance? Safety? Whether you are working in a nursing home, adult day center, or other type of senior care center, your facility is home to your participants for part or all of their day. Although nothing can really take the place of home, many adaptations can make the people in your care feel more at ease.

Most of us would prefer not to think about it, but the truth is that some physical decline accompanies aging in even the healthiest of adults. Sensory losses, decreased muscle strength and reflex time, and diminished energy levels are all normal parts of growing older. When these declines are coupled with Alzheimer's disease and related disorders, a person becomes even less able to handle the tasks of daily living.

A person's physical capabilities and disabilities can greatly affect his or her ability to cope with the environment and to participate in activities. People in the field of aging look at the physical environment as a therapeutic tool. By paying attention to the physical and social environment of a facility, we can maximize a person's strengths, self-respect, and dignity.

We were very fortunate to have the opportunity to design our building to fit the needs of the older population. You may not have this luxury, but adaptations can be made in any building that will increase the quality of life for your participants.

Safety

You undoubtedly have a number of safeguards and procedures in place to protect your participants. The environment needs to be designed or adapted to balance the greatest amount of independence with the least amount of risk. A tamperproof switch on stoves, antiscald devices on faucets, nonskid floors in plain colors, no throw rugs, call buttons in restrooms, and protection in sockets will help to accomplish this goal.

For people with Alzheimer's disease, the desire to wander can be intense. An area that allows free movement in a secure setting can greatly lessen agitation and the inclination to escape. Our outdoor wandering courtyard offers a safe setting that accommodates such behaviors. The layout is a loop, which suggests a continuous forward motion with no decision points. All of the flooring in the corridor and path is the same to eliminate visual cliffing (i.e., misjudgment in depth perception that can be caused by contrasting colors).

Minimizing Distractions

Tuning out distractions takes energy—energy that some of your participants can't spare. By cutting down on distractions, you can reduce confusion and enhance a person's capabilities. Noise, crowding, glare, foul or unfamiliar odors, and unrelated activity can interrupt the thought processes. Even moderately impaired people can overload from too much distraction and may withdraw, have outbursts, or attempt to escape from a confusing or overwhelming setting.

Interruptions such as people entering and leaving the room, phones ringing, people conversing in the hall, and so on should be minimized whenever possible. Outside noises like street traffic and lawn mowers, or inside ones like air conditioners will also have an effect. Even normal levels of light and noise may be sensed as extreme by some of your participants. Sometimes a change in light sources or a decrease in noise will dramatically alter a person's ability to concentrate, converse, or complete a task. When such distractions happen, your staff should understand that disruption may occur in ongoing activities or conversations.

Sensory Cues

As sensory losses progress, multiple sensory cues, (i.e., providing the same information in a variety of ways) can maintain a measure of independence. For example, the way to the restroom can be marked by a sign with a directional arrow, a line on the floor to the restroom, and a contrasting color of the restroom door.

As vision fades, high levels of consistent light from multiple sources— incandescent, fluorescent, and natural whenever possible—will compensate for diminishing sight. Watch, however, for glare or harsh lighting, which may cause distraction or agitation. Visual contrasts that increase the distinction between objects will heighten older adults' ability to distinguish things in their environment. Signs should be large with dark letters on a white background.

Many older participants have hearing impairments and find the noise of large groups upsetting. Carpeting can dampen extraneous noises. Drop ceilings with acoustical tile can also lessen noise levels, encouraging more socialization among participants.

Accessibility

Hand rails, ramps, and grab bars throughout your facility will help your participants to maintain independent mobility. Lever style handles instead of knobs on doors, faucets, and windows will make manipulation easier. Special attention should be given to make restroom areas accessible and safe.

Familiarity

As we said earlier, whether for the daytime hours or around the clock, your facility is home to your participants. We try to encourage this at-home feeling, by allowing people to do the things they would do in their own home—make coffee in the morning, sit quietly with the paper, chat with friends, or work in the garden.

You can do other things to make your center feel more like home. We refer to our "living room" as just that—a living room not a lounge. Our facility is decorated like a home instead of an institution. Our kitchen includes equipment that would be found in a home, and is as accessible as we can make it. Whenever possible, we try to offer a sense of familiarity and continuity. For example, a drinking fountain should look like a traditional drinking fountain and not an abstract sculpture.

Individual Adaptations

No one adaptation will help everyone. As always, your staff need to be familiar with your participants and sensitive to individual needs. Check to see that the appropriate people wear working hearing aids and glasses. Converse at the person's eye level to promote eye contact and to eliminate neck strain. Be sure that the temperature is comfortable—an older person in a wheelchair may feel much colder than a younger staff member moving around.

These are just a few of the ways that you can make your center more user-friendly. Take a walk through your facility and look at everything with a fresh perspective. If this were your home (and it is for at least part of the day), what changes would you want to make? Although Dorothy was right when she said there's no place like home, a few adaptations can help participants feel that they have a home away from home.

Chapter 5
Beyond Baskets and Beads:
Planning Your Activity Program

*First thing in the morning, Flo makes herself some coffee. She takes
a cup to the living room where she enjoys it over the morning paper.
Later, she will probably do some gardening. Or maybe it would be a
nice day to see if her friend Bessie wants to take a walk. She'll set the
table and prepare lunch. Then there's her book discussion group, and
it will nearly be time for dinner. Many people would say that Flo, at
age 80, is fortunate to be able to live her life in much the same way
that she did when she was younger. We think Flo would agree. The
only difference is that she now enjoys these activities in our Center.
Our greatest source of pride is that people like Flo can continue to
make choices, do the things they enjoy, plan their own days—in short,
to get on with the business of living—with us.*

Activities can add so much to your facility. They offer opportunities to socialize,
to learn new things, and to revisit past pleasures. They can be something
special to look forward to or a comfortable part of the regular routine. There
can be room for solo pursuits as well as group participation.

What activities should not be, however, are central events strung together
by empty hours of waiting. We've seen dayrooms full of people assembled at

nine o'clock in the morning because bingo is scheduled for eleven. These men and women must spend two hours of their lives doing absolutely nothing to play a half-hour round of a game they may not even like!

By using the participant-centered approach, the older adults in our Center choose how they will fill their days. Even in the case of people with significant impairments, we try to respect their choices as much as possible. While we're not going to allow a gentleman with Alzheimer's disease the choice of wandering off the property or out into the street, we *will* find a volunteer or staff member to accompany him on a walk to fulfill his need for movement.

Last February, Joe wanted to have a barbecue in the 35°F rain. It would have been easy to say no. Instead, Joe and one of our intrepid volunteers bundled up, fired up the grill, and made hamburgers for everyone. It was a treat!

Another time, Gary, the big-band lover we mentioned earlier, wanted to dance. One of our directors, who also loves to dance, dropped what she was doing and danced with him for half an hour to the delight of everyone. She probably took paperwork home that night, but it was a small price to pay for a memory like that.

In one week, our adult day center activities included the following:

- Swimming with a volunteer for one participant
- Making pizza and shortcake (no one wanted the regular menu)
- Current events discussion
- Planting seeds for a vegetable garden
- Folding dish towels for the Center
- Making crafts for our Fall Festival
- Storytelling
- Playing ball in the courtyard and hallways
- Podiatry screening
- And so on...

Some of the things we do fall into the category of "planned activities." Others are what a particular person needed or wanted to do that day. We may coax a hesitant person to join an activity, but he or she is *never* coerced or forced. Whatever a person's physical or mental condition, it's still his or her life.

On the other hand, although we don't tell people what they must do, we also do not tell them what they *can't* do.

Fred wanted to enroll in a course called "Reading Road Maps." In all honesty, no one believed that he had the capabilities to handle this course, but enroll he did. To everyone's surprise, Fred did well enough to earn a "B" and expressed interest in learning to use the computer. We were able to get a computer for our adult day center, and a student is now tutoring him.

In many cases, our most successful "activities" are just an extension of real life. For example, cooking is a favorite. Everyone takes a part in the preparation, including participants in wheelchairs. One of the women was so thrilled to help in the kitchen because she "isn't allowed to" at home. We really don't care if a dish gets broken or the towels aren't folded correctly. *We care that our participants feel needed.* Many of our participants have brought in their favorite recipes to share with us. One man's family was amazed that their tough-guy dad would cook, but he was especially proud of his ham and bean recipe and shared it with his "other" family. At one picnic, our participants made three different kinds of potato salad because everyone wanted to make his or her favorite.

Gardening is another popular activity for many people at our Center. This year, we tried out our green thumbs in our raised garden. By positioning the garden at waist level, anyone who wants to can take part. This is an activity where so many of our participants shine. Some had Victory gardens (a WWII term for gardens grown to produce one's own food and thus conserve resources), while others have raised vegetables and flowers their whole lives. Our participants are the experts, while our generally black-thumbed staff are the novices who can learn from them.

On the other hand, crafts, which serve as a cornerstone for many activity programs, are relatively rare in our Center. This is not to say that we don't do crafts. Some have worked well and we will repeat them. Undoubtedly, we'll continue to try some new ideas to expand our craft repertoire. In addition, some of our participants have done crafts their whole lives and still enjoy them. As a rule, though, craft projects are few and far between for us. There are several reasons for this.

1. We've tried them, and they've been met with little enthusiasm among our participants.

2. Many of the standard craft activities seem inappropriate for adults. Even titles like Cutting Snowflakes and Making Paper Chains strike us as demeaning. For example, one of our regular participants is an 80-year-old ex-miner who spent much of his adult life caring for a disabled son. Do we really expect him to spend his remaining years on Torn Paper Art?

3. Fine motor skills and vision aren't as good as they once were, making it more difficult for participants to meet with success. Many would be aware of and embarrassed by a shoddy end result.

4. The activity directors we surveyed for this project cited arts and crafts as one of their biggest problem areas.

If you were to visit our Center, you would not find a roomful of people making a popsicle stick and glitter project. You *would* see a group of individuals each going his or her own way. Lenny might be reading the paper while Martha and Julie work on preparing lunch. Millie could be folding laundry. Fred might be at his map class, while Edna visits with Flash, our pet therapy dog. Joe and Rita both have plans for the afternoon—he has line dancing, while she never misses the noontime sing-along. Ted, a doer all his life, stays active by helping with dishes, yard work, or maintenance projects.

When one of our most popular programs like the Armchair Traveler is going on, you might find most of our participants in one place enjoying a group activity. Chances are, though, one or two would be out walking with a volunteer or reading quietly because they were "not in the mood" to sit through a program. That's just fine with us.

On the following pages we've listed almost 100 of our favorite activity suggestions. Some may work well in your facility, while others will not, but we hope that you'll find at least a few new favorites to add spice to your program.

If you've read other activity manuals, you will notice that a couple of commonly seen items are missing from ours. We haven't listed participant to staff ratios because we don't know your participants *or* your staff. We believe that only someone familiar with the individuals involved can make an accurate determination of ratio. We also have omitted preparation times. Your preparation time will depend on how elaborate a program you are planning, and the experience of the staff and volunteers involved. When possible, we have included the sources where we buy our materials. Activities are also cross-indexed in the Appendix to simplify finding the particular type of activity you need. You may find that you use our activity ideas as jumping off points, and will want to take note of any variations and adaptations that work for you.

On page 35 you will find our model for a participant-centered activity program. Each small circle represents one of our participants, including his or her needs and preferences. All of the small circles feed into the hub of the wheel, which represents our overall activity program. As you can see, the small circles "drive" the central one, thus creating a participant-centered program. We hope that this manual will help you to start or to maintain such a program for your facility.

Our role is not to tell people what to do, but rather to offer a variety of choices and adaptations that allow them to find continued satisfaction in their lives. This means helping them to stay active, to feel useful, and even to take the occasional calculated risk. The heaviest burden on anyone is having nothing at all to carry.

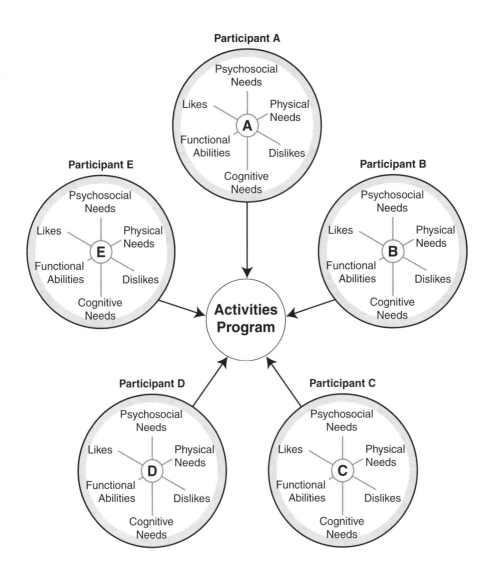

Participant-Centered Activities Program Model
The activities program is designed to fit the interests and plan of care for each individual.

Favorite Activities

These activities provide important therapeutic benefits for participants. Some focus more on mental stimulation while others engage participants in physical activity. All provide opportunities for socialization and enjoyment. Whether you wish to improve participants' self-esteem, encourage reminiscence and sharing, or simply provide a fun, novel experience, there's an activity for that. The index can help you choose the activity type.

Advent or Event Calendar

Anticipates upcoming events and holidays
Keeps participants oriented

While traditionally associated with Christmas, an advent/event calendar can be used to look forward to any special event. (The word advent literally means a "coming" or an "approach.")

Christmas Advent calendars are readily available in the late autumn. For other events, a large version can be made by cutting three-sided "windows" in a piece of poster board and backing it on a second piece. Windows can be raised to reveal a picture, message, fact, or small prize. Include the date on each window, and have your participants take turns opening a window each day leading up to your special event.

In addition to holidays, an event calendar can be used as any special day approaches. Examples could include a landmark birthday for one of your participants, an open house or anniversary celebration at your facility, and any other day that deserves fanfare.

Materials: Purchased advent calendar, or supplies to make custom-made calendar (e.g., posterboard, tape, razor knife, pictures, messages, prizes)

Alphabetically Speaking

Stimulates memory
Encourages teamwork among the group

Players try to think of a word for each letter of the alphabet to fit a given category. For example in the category of "cars," the first three answers might be Austin, Buick, and Cadillac.

Materials: A large wipe-off board or flip chart, markers to record answers

Aquariums

Adds beauty for everyone to enjoy
Offers an opportunity to nurture

Nearly everyone can appreciate the tranquil pleasure of watching an aquarium. A pet store can help you purchase the needed supplies: aquarium,

gravel, filters/pump, plants, fish food, and compatible fish. Interested participants can take satisfaction in helping to care for the fish.
Materials: Aquarium starter kit, fish

Armchair Traveler

One of our most popular activities
Gives participants a chance to "see the world"
Encourages memories and discussions of past travels
Guests are invited to share slides, photos or videos of their travels, highlighting local customs, foods, and so on. Activity can be planned to fit any time frame, with some portion allotted for questions and discussion. A large map with pertinent areas flagged with pins and a world globe can be helpful.
Materials: Appropriate audio and video equipment, maps/globe

Auction

Combines the challenge of shopping for a bargain with the fun of getting "something for nothing"
Participants bid to buy small items of their choice. Donated or purchased items could include puzzle or word search books, stationery and envelopes, cookies or candy, costume jewelry, or knick knacks. These are to be displayed before the start of the auction.

Each player is given a paper with an equal amount of photocopied play money bills. Each item is sold to the highest bidder who then crosses off the amount of money spent from his or her sheet. Ties for highest bid can be broken by a roll of the dice with the high cast taking the item.
Materials: Auction items, photocopies of "money," pencils, dice

Balloon Volleyball

Fun for everyone
Works for large or small groups
Perfect for intergenerational activities
Players can be arranged in a circle with a common goal of keeping the balloon from touching the floor. A variation is to set up two teams facing one another who try to keep the balloon off the floor on their side of a dividing line. Toss in a balloon and begin.
Materials: Balloons or balloon ball.

Best-Seller Book Review

Highly motivating for lifelong readers
Can be tailored to target areas of interest

    Best-selling books are read aloud by chapter or section, then discussed among the group. Props mentioned in the book can spark additional interest. Some books which have been popular for us include: *All I Ever Needed to Know I Learned in Kindergarten*, *Having Our Say* by the Delaney Sisters, *Bridges of Madison County*, *Angels Among Us*, and anything by Erma Bombeck.

    Materials: Books, donated or from library

Birdhouse Carpentry

Craft with a purpose
Popular with men and women alike

    Birdhouses are a popular craft because of the usefulness of the finished product. Identify a place to hang the birdhouses in advance. Parts can be cut out by experienced volunteers, staff and participants, or precut kits can be used. Detail painting may be difficult and can lead to frustration; we prefer staining and/or varnishing.

    Materials: Wooden parts, nails, sandpaper, stain or varnish, appropriate tools. Kits can be purchased at many craft stores or ordered through:

Briggs Corporation	Sea Bay Game Company
Box 1698	77 Cliffwood Avenue, Suite 1D
Des Moines, IA 50309–1698	Cliffwood, NJ 07721
Phone (800) 307-1744	Phone (800) 568-0188
Fax (800) 222-1996	Fax (732) 583-7284
http://www.briggscorp.com	http://www.seabaygame.com

Birdwatchers

Activities for bird lovers

    Whether as casual observers or more serious birdwatchers, most people can appreciate the beauty and grace of our feathered friends. A few activities to spark this interest include

Guess the Bird

The group leader describes a particular bird and asks the group to name it. Descriptions may include physical description, habitat, and even songs or calls. Group members can then be invited to describe a bird for the group. Depending on your participants, you may want to show pictures of the birds.

Bird Feeder

Mount a bird feeder near a window. Participants can take turns making sure that the feeder is filled each day. You may want to keep a notebook nearby to

record the "visitors" you can identify, and/or a good bird identification book. In warm weather, try providing a bird bath in a visible location.
Materials: Bird feeder, bird seed

Bird Silhouettes
Prepare silhouettes of distinctive birds from a bird book, and ask the participants to identify each. Keep the book handy so that you can show the picture of each bird.
Materials: Bird book, construction paper, glue

Bird Talk
Contact your local Audubon Society or bird club to arrange for a visit from an expert. If you have a bird sanctuary or rescue in the area, their personnel may be willing to visit with some of their charges.
Related activities: *Birdhouse Carpentry, Pine Cone Bird Feeders*

Breakfast at Tiffany's
Adds a touch of elegance to any day
Brings back memories of special days gone by
A great photo opportunity for everyone
This activity originated to commemorate the anniversary of Tiffany's jewelry store, but creates a sophisticated atmosphere anytime. Have a continental breakfast of coffee, tea, and pastries served on borrowed lace tablecloths and china. Invite participants to wear their favorite finery, including "all that glitters." Borrow rhinestone jewelry and other accessories.
Materials: Borrowed finery, refreshments, camera and film

Butter Making
Fun to make, with a tasty end result for all to share
Half a cup of heavy whipping cream and one tablespoon of sour cream are placed in a container with a tight lid. Participants take turns shaking the container for a few minutes. The resulting lump of butter can be spread on bread and shared. This activity will easily stimulate discussion of butter-churning and other food preparation from "the old days."
Materials: Sour cream, heavy whipping cream, container, kitchen utensils, bread or crackers

Calendar Party
Wraps up the year with reminders of past celebrations
Tables are decorated to celebrate a theme for each month of the year. For example, January—New Year's or snowflakes; February—Valentine's or President's Day; March—St. Patrick's Day or the March lion and lamb. Table

coverings, napkins, favors, and desserts served can all reflect the table theme. A song for each month could provide the entertainment. If this activity is planned in advance, decorations and tableware can be saved from holidays throughout the year.

Materials: Paper plates and napkins, utensils, decorations, favors, desserts

Candlelight Christmas

Brings back the holiday celebrations of a simpler time

This observance of the Christmas season includes fresh pine decorations, scented candles, and other old-fashioned decorations. Seasonal poems, stories and carols are told. Refreshments like cookies, punch, hot cider, cocoa, or eggnog complete the picture.

Materials: Pine decorations and candles, refreshments

Celebrity Chefs

Gives each participant a day in the spotlight and a chance to play host
A perfect opportunity to bring community members into your facility

One or more participants or guests volunteer to cook for an audience. Each chef brings in his or her favorite recipe and demonstrates expertise in the kitchen by cooking for the group. Everyone shares in the results.

Materials: Ingredients, kitchen utensils/appliances as needed

Children's Book Project

Combines artistic expression with the satisfaction of helping children

Basic pictures of objects representing each letter of the alphabet are drawn with a permanent fabric marker on muslin squares. Participants paint the pictures with fabric paint. (Tape wax paper to the table to protect it, then tape squares to the wax paper for easier handling.) When dry, the squares are placed face-to-face and sewn, then turned right side out. Three or four squares are sewn together to make a book. Books can be donated to local schools or day centers.

Adaptation: If a painted book is too challenging for some participants, a simpler version can be made. Pictures are cut from magazines for each letter of the alphabet, then pasted into a scrapbook and labeled. For example, the "A" page might include a picture of an apple, an airplane, and an ant. This simpler version still allows the makers the satisfaction of making something useful for children.

Materials: Muslin squares, approximately 9" each, permanent markers, fabric paint, wax paper, tape, sewing machine; for adaptation: scrapbook, old magazines, scissors, paste, pens

Chocolate-Dipped Strawberries

A delicious treat that everyone can help to prepare
    Participants help to clean the berries. Chocolate is melted, the berry is dipped in chocolate, and placed on wax paper to harden.
    Materials: Fresh strawberries; melting chocolate (available where candy-making supplies are sold); double boiler and stove or microwave and Pyrex container; kitchen utensils (e.g., tongs, skewers, mixing spoon); wax paper

Choose Your Own Adventure

An enjoyable exercise in decision making
Highlights a flair for the dramatic
    This series of books describe fantasy adventures in a variety of settings such as under the sea or in a space colony. Players act the part of the characters and make choices that determine the outcome of the story.
    Materials: *Choose Your Own Adventure* books (184 titles were published, primarily through the 1980s. Although currently out-of-print, used book stores and amazon.com are good places to look.)

Clothing Theme Days

The only limit is your imagination
Brightens up an "ordinary" day
    Participants and staff wear clothing to match the theme of the day. These just-for-fun days are great photo opportunities and promote group cohesiveness. Have extras on hand so that everyone can choose to participate. Some examples are: Crazy or Ugly Tie Day (especially appropriate for Father's Day), Hat Day, Backwards Day, Purple Day, Big Earring Day
    Materials: Extra articles to fit the theme, camera and film

Community Connections

Integrates your facility with the community
Helps participants to maintain community ties
    Your participants need to know that they are a part of the community. Activities that bring the community into your facility as well as those that take your participants out will help to foster this feeling. They will also help to maintain or increase community support for your work.
    Many of the activities in this chapter offer the opportunity to bring the community and your facility together. Some additional ideas for fostering community connections include the following:

   • *Ask community members to present programs*. People who may not be able to volunteer on a regular basis can often give a couple of hours. They may be willing to talk about their jobs or hobbies, demonstrate skills, or show special collections.

• *Invite the community to your programs*. If you are having a program of general interest, whether it be a poetry reading or a lecture on local history, open your program to the public.

• *Hold special events open to the public*. Craft festivals, ethnic days, holiday celebrations, and so on can greatly increase the community's awareness of your facility.

• *Have an "open door" policy*. Families, friends, and community members should feel welcome in your facility as much as possible.

• *Look for opportunities to take your participants into the community*. Your trips will depend on your participants and budget, but it is important to plan outings into the community whether it's visits to the mall, the art gallery or the ball park.

• *Offer your facilities to other groups*. If you have space, make your center available to community organizations. Can the school hold its science fair there or the choral group its holiday concert? They are sure to appreciate the invitation.

Creative Writing

Stimulates language skills
Offers an outlet for creative expression

Just as some of your participants will respond to art or music programs, others will find satisfaction in expressing themselves through the written word. Creative writing can be stimulated in a number of ways, depending on the interests and functional levels of your participants. Stories may be told to a staff member or volunteer who writes them down, making complete sentences when needed but keeping the ideas and style intact.

Keep each writer's work in a binder or portfolio. Special works can be bound into books at an office store. Participants may want to read their works to a group, or share them with their families.

Some ideas for encouraging creative writing include

Story Starters

The beginning or topic sentence of a story is given, and writers are asked to complete the work. You can use your own ideas, find some on the Internet, or purchase resources at a school supply store. A simpler method is to read sentences with key words missing and ask participants to fill in the blanks.

Themed Stories

A theme is suggested for exploration by the writers. For example, you might suggest "The Biggest Snowstorm I Remember" or "My Best Birthday."

Picture Themes

A picture of an object is shown. Participants are encouraged to write about the picture or related experiences. The picture can be attached to the finished work.

Letter or Card Writing

Some participants may not be interested in stories or essays, but may be glad to write letters to friends and family or create cards for special occasions.
   Related activity: Pen Pals

Group Story Writing

The leader starts the story. Each member of the group takes a turn at continuing the story until a conclusion is reached. Record the story, then transcribe to written form.

Current Events Update

Keeps participants attuned to world happenings
Continues a lifelong practice for many
   Highlights of a local or national newspaper are read to the group, focusing on headlines, weather, advice columns, local events, sports, and other areas of interest to the participants. Discussion is encouraged. A "what happened on this date" feature can evoke memories and reminiscence.
   Materials: Daily paper

Dance, Dance, Dance

A great physical activity disguised as pure fun
Enjoyable for dancers and audience alike
   Whether square, line, or ballroom style, dancing is a very popular activity and can be adapted to allow nearly anyone to take part. People in wheelchairs can join the dance with a little assistance, and onlookers can clap their hands, tap their toes, or just enjoy the music. Tunes from the 30s and 40s may be especially well-received, but variety can keep the interest level high. If there are more women than men, volunteers, such as a group from a local fraternity, can fill in the gender gap. (Many women won't mind a same-sex partner, either.)
   Materials: Music

Dartball

Baseball with darts—a sure winner for sports fans

Make a dartboard out of a 4-foot by 8-foot piece of foam insulation or use a large purchased board. Attach pieces of paper on which are printed appropriate baseball terms such as "single," "double," "home run," and "out." (A more elaborate version can be made to resemble a baseball diamond.) Mount the dartboard in a low-traffic area, and observe extra safety measures, including one-on-one supervision for dart throwers. Two teams of players take turns throwing darts to score. A player throws until he is safely on base or out. As in baseball, three outs end the team's "at bat."

Materials: A 4-by-8–foot insulation board, darts, flip chart for keeping score

Day of Peace (Martin Luther King, Jr. Day)

Honors an American hero
Recognizes the contribution of King to the Civil Rights Movement

This observance honors the memory of Dr. Martin Luther King, Jr., while celebrating the cultural diversity of America. Activities can include readings from Dr. King's "I Have a Dream" speech and a discussion of his contribution to our society. The theme of peace can be carried throughout your facility by decorating with peace signs, doves, and other appropriate symbols.

Materials: Book on Martin Luther King, Jr., decorations

Dice Tee Ball

Baseball fans love this indoor version of the all-American game

In this purchased game, a large foam die is placed on a batting tee. The die is connected to the tee by a piece of elastic. A "baseball diamond" mat is placed on the floor, with the tee at home base. Players take turns hitting the die, which indicates how to advance the figurine "players." Any number can join the game. Players may also decide to advance to the bases themselves rather than using figures.

Materials: Game pieces include a batting tee, bat, foam die with elastic, baseball diamond mat, and figures. Available from:

Sea Bay Game Company
77 Cliffwood Avenue, Suite 1D
Cliffwood, NJ 07721
Phone (800) 568-0188
Fax (732) 583-7284
http://www.seabaygame.com

Dirt Cake

Tastes a lot better than it sounds
A treat and a conversation piece all in one

This novelty recipe becomes even more novel when served in a large flowerpot or small individual ones (new only, of course), and decorated with flowers and gummy worms.

Recipe: Mix together in large bowl:
  1 cup powdered sugar
  8 ounce package of cream cheese
Mix in separate bowl:
  2 small packages instant vanilla pudding
  3 cups milk
  1 teaspoon vanilla
Combine mixtures in a large bowl and mix in:
  12 ounce container of whipped topping
Crumble one large package of chocolate sandwich cookies

In a 9x13x2–inch pan, spread one half of cookie crumbs. Spread mixture over bottom layer, then top with remainder of crumbs.

Materials: Ingredients, kitchen utensils, flowerpots, decorations (if desired)

Easter Eggs

Perfect for intergenerational activities
A traditional springtime favorite

Remembered by many from childhood, Easter egg coloring is most enjoyable when shared with others, whether it's a Brownie troop or a college sorority. Eggs are hard-boiled, then dyed with food coloring, purchased egg dyes, or natural vegetable dyes. Check your library for a book on making your own natural dyes. A protected work area, old clothes, and egg holders (which may be made from wire hangers) will ensure that only eggs are dyed.

Materials: Hard-boiled eggs, dye, utensils

Election Day

Allows citizens to exercise their right to vote
Increases awareness of national events

Make sure that your participants who will vote are registered by the necessary deadline, know the location of their polling place, and check the regulations governing absentee ballots. During the election season, focus discussions on the candidates and issues. On Election Day, decorate the room with red, white, and blue

streamers, flags, and/or balloons. Set up a mock voting booth where partici-pants can cast ballots and learn about various aspects of the voting procedure. Be sure to discuss the results of the actual election the following day.

Materials: Balloons, crepe paper, flags, absentee ballots

Fiesta

A celebration of the culture of Mexico
Makes a special Cinco de Mayo celebration

Decorations, costumes, music, and foods from Mexico are just a few of the ways to create the fiesta atmosphere. An added touch is piñatas made from paper bags. Decorate the bags with crepe paper and stickers, fill them with candy or small prizes, and staple the bags closed. These piñatas can be sus-pended from the ceiling and broken open with a stick in the traditional way.

Materials: Decorations, foods, piñata supplies—paper bags, candy or prizes, decorations for bags, a stick to break piñata

Five-Minute Mysteries

An enjoyable way to practice problem-solving skills
Taps into the popularity of mystery stories among older adults

Five Minute Mysteries is a book of short cases of mystery and mayhem. Stories are read aloud, and possible solutions to the cases are proposed and discussed. Two sequels (*Further Five-Minute Mysteries* and *More Five-Minute Mysteries*) are also available from the publisher.

Materials: *Five-Minute Mysteries* book(s), available from:
Running Press Book Publishers
125 South 22nd Street
Philadelphia, PA 19103-4399
Phone: (800) 345-5359

Flower Arranging

A treat for flower lovers
Results are a source of pride and pleasure

Invite a local florist to teach a flower-arranging class. Prior to the class, encourage participants to share their experiences and memories associated with flowers. If you grow flowers at your facility, this is a perfect time to use them. Plans for your ar-rangements, such as a location in your center or a donation to someone in the community, can also be made.

Materials: Fresh and/or dried flowers and greens, vases or baskets, floral foam, shears

Fly a Kite

A traditional spring ritual of childhood, as much fun now as it was then
Makes an ideal intergenerational activity

Go fly a kite! Participants enjoy the beauty and freedom of flying and watching kites in the great outdoors. Everyone can help with assembling the kite, tying on the tail, and holding the string as it soars.

Materials: Kite kit

Folk Tales and Heroes

Well-loved tales which always deserve another telling
A part of America's shared culture

Popular folklore stories like Paul Bunyan, Pecos Bill, and Johnny Appleseed are read or told, with accompanying songs and videos when available.

Materials: Stories, videos, music

Food Glorious Food

Activities relating to food are the absolute favorites in our Center for many reasons: the familiarity of the activity, a love of cooking and baking, the feelings of usefulness, the enjoyment of the end result, and so on. (Of course, your knowledge of your participants' dietary needs will have to be taken into consideration on any food-related activity.)

Some of our favorite cooking activities have been listed separately in this chapter. The possibilities are limitless, but we'd like to offer a few other ideas for incorporating food preparation into your activity program:

Meal and Snack Preparation

While not a planned activity, helping with daily food preparation can be very rewarding for some people. Look for ways to include these participants. Some may be able to make the salad or sandwiches, while others may be happy to set tables or help with cleanup.

Barbecues

Everything tastes better grilled outside—even in February! Picnics are also a welcome diversion, even if the "picnic" has to be eaten in the dining room.

Bonfire Parties

We never outgrow the fun of roasting hot dogs or marshmallows over an open fire. Extra supervision and attention to safety are needed, of course.

Candy Making

Fudge, caramels, peanut brittle, and hard candy are all relatively easy and inexpensive. An old-fashioned taffy pull is a bit messy but lots of fun and sure to bring back memories.

Canning, Jelly and Jam Making
Chances are that some of your participants have done this many times and may welcome the chance to try it again. You'll need experienced staff or volunteers on hand for this project.

New Food Party
With the availability of exotic fruits and vegetables and other specialty foods, a tasting party can be arranged. Be as adventurous as you dare.

Cookie Baking and Decorating
This is especially appropriate for the holidays and special events, or when a children's group will be visiting to enjoy the results.

Bread Baking
Nothing beats the therapeutic value of pounding and kneading the dough when you bake the "old-fashioned" way.

Homemade Ice Cream
Borrow an ice cream freezer and make your own. (For a simpler version, see *Ice Cream Making.*)

Ice Cream Party
Supply ice cream (homemade or store bought) and lots of toppings. Let everyone create a fantasy sundae.

Popcorn
Pop it for movie nights or string it for the Christmas tree.

Gingerbread Houses
Whether simple or elaborate, these traditional favorites are great group projects, especially when you invite some children to help with the decorating.

Fourth of July Sparklers

What would the Fourth be without fireworks? Prior to activity, check the local fireworks ordinances. Participants gather in a clear outside area, with plenty of room left between people. Containers of water are placed every few feet to extinguish sparklers. Each participant is given a sparkler to hold. Because of the risk of burns, one-on-one supervision will be needed for many participants. Playing patriotic music will add to the festivities.

Materials: Sparklers, lighter, music

Giant Crossword

A group approach to a popular pastime
Stimulates memory, word retrieval, problem solving
    Copy any puzzle from a crossword book onto large, 11-by-17–inch paper squares taped together, or posterboard, making 3-inch by 3-inch grid squares. Black squares should be painted or covered with black paper.
    Materials: Paper or posterboard, paint, crossword puzzle book

Group Painting

A group artistic effort, resulting in a sense of accomplishment for all
    Invite a local artist to help with this project. A sketch is made on the canvas first. Each participant paints a portion of the picture, which is then matted and framed for display in the center or the community.
    Materials: Painting supplies: canvas, paint, dropcloths, brushes, mat, frame

Handwriting Analysis

A self-esteem booster
Celebrates individuality
    Bring in a graphologist to examine your participants' handwriting. If no one is available, have a staff member do some homework on the subject, and give it a whirl. Each person writes his or her name and a short sentence on a sheet of paper. Share all of the positive results with the group.
    Materials: Paper, pens

Hatching Chicks

A perfect harbinger of spring
The pleasure of watching new life come into the world
    Contact a 4H club or poultry farm in your area about a chick hatching program. They provide the incubator and the eggs, which take about 21 days to hatch. Be sure to arrange for a home for the chicks before you begin. The incubator must be placed in a safe area away from drafts where the temperature will not change. Participants choose eggs, number and name them, and wait to see whose egg hatches first.
    Materials: Incubator, fertilized eggs, food for hatchlings

Holiday Lighting Ceremony

Brings your participants together with other community members
A beautiful observance of the holidays
    Community groups are invited into your facility for this lighting ceremony. You may choose to light a menorah for Hanukkah, a mishumaa for Kwanzaa

and/or a tree for Christmas. This can create a special interfaith program for the holidays. The guests meet in a darkened area, appropriate verse or passages may be read, and a member of the group is invited to light the first candle of the menorah, mishumaa and/or the Christmas tree. Seasonal music and refreshments complete the program.

Materials: Menorah, Mishumaa, decorated Christmas tree, readings, music, refreshments

Ice Cream Making

Tastes as good as the old-fashioned kind, but made a whole new way
Fun to make and to share

Participants in groups of two or three are given the ingredients and supplies to make ice cream.

Recipe: In a one quart resealable plastic storage bag, place $\frac{1}{2}$ cup whole milk (or light cream), 1 tablespoon sugar, and 1 teaspoon vanilla; seal bag. Fill a one-gallon resealable plastic storage bag two-thirds full with crushed ice; add 7 tablespoons salt. Place small bag inside large bag and seal. Pass the bag among the participants and shake it for five to seven minutes. Makes one cup of soft-serve ice milk.

Materials: Quart and gallon sealable bags, ingredients, crushed ice, salt, kitchen utensils

Impressionistic/Abstract Art

Artistic expression for everyone
Stimulates the imagination

Artists are given good quality watercolor paper or linen finish posterboard, brush or stick sponges, and nontoxic, washable paints. Participants are shown examples of impressionist and abstract art to stimulate their imaginations. Mat and frame the work. Display in your facility or community center.

Materials: Paper or posterboard, sponges and/or brushes, paints, and supplies are available in most art and craft stores or from:

Pickett Enterprises	S&S Worldwide
P.O. Box 3410	P.O. Box 513, 75 Mill Street
Wilsonville, OR 97070	Colchester, CT 06415
Phone (800) 500-5641	Phone (800) 243-9232
Fax (800) 449-2188	Fax (800) 566-6678
http://www.pickettenterprises.com	http://www.snswwide.com

Indoor Herb Garden

An opportunity to show off green thumbs
Adds a touch of home to your facility

New and experienced gardeners will enjoy growing fresh herbs like basil, dill, and rosemary in a year-round window garden. Plant each herb in a separate clay pot, labeled with the name of the herb. Pots should be placed in trays lined with about an inch of pebbles. Add enough water to cover the pebbles. Place trays near a sunny window, with an instruction card nearby. When your herbs flourish, they will add a pleasing aroma to the area, and can be used for cooking projects as well.

Materials: Seeds, pots, soil, tray, pebbles, labels, instructions

Intergenerational Activities

Intergenerational activities should be an integral part of any participant-centered activities program. Many of our activities can be adapted to be intergenerational. Some additional ways to bring a variety of community members into your facility include the following:

Adopted or Foster Grandparents Program

Contact a local school or church to see if you can arrange to match up children with "grandparents."

Grandparents Day

Have a celebration which includes inviting grandchildren and "adopted" grandchildren to join in the fun.

Scout Troops

Many Boy Scout or Girl Scout troops will be happy to come to your facility for special programs or as regular visitors.

School Shows

Your local schools can be a rich source of entertainment for your participants, many of whom will delight in just seeing the children. Find out when your schools hold special events like concerts, talent shows, science fairs, and so forth. You may be able to arrange to have a mini-concert or exhibit at your facility or, if you have the room, might even offer to host an entire event.

Holidays

Invite children in whenever possible. They can help decorate the Christmas tree, light the menorah, light the mishumaa for a Kwanzaa celebration, dye Easter eggs, or put on a Halloween parade. Children are a guaranteed crowd pleaser for holiday celebrations.

Youth Groups

Get acquainted with the groups in your area. High school service clubs, church groups, fraternities, sororities, and many others can be wonderful sources of volunteers.

Jeopardy

An easy-to-read version of the television favorite
Questions can be adapted to fit varying levels of functioning/areas of interest
This large-format version of *Jeopardy* tests knowledge and recall just like the popular television and board game. While this game takes a fair amount of preparation, it is one of our most popular activities and well worth the time investment. Periodic updates will be needed to add new categories and questions. A large game board is designed with at least six slots for categories across the top and five spaces for questions beneath each category. Questions are placed on 3-by-5–inch cards. A *Jeopardy* board game can be used for format and ideas for questions, which can be adapted to meet your group's needs. For participants with more significant impairments, photos or pictures may be used instead of questions. Have prizes on hand for the winner(s).

Materials: Posterboard, construction paper, questions cards, prizes. The *Jeopardy* board game is available at many toy stores, or from:
Sea Bay Game Company
77 Cliffwood Avenue, Suite 1D
Cliffwood, NJ 07721
Phone (800) 568-0188
Fax (732) 583-7284
http://www.seabaygame.com

Lifestories

Game of shared experiences and memories
This game includes a playing board and subject cards intended to trigger memories of life experiences.

Materials: *Lifestories* game (about $30). May be ordered from:
areyougame.com
2030 Harrison Street
San Francisco, CA 94110
Phone (800) 471-0641
Fax (415) 503-0085
http://www.areyougame.com

Memory Book/Memory Wallet

Comforting to anxious participants
A treasury of personal memories to keep nearby

Memory books and memory wallets are collections of personal information and photographs and may include information about a participant's likes and dislikes, family members, and so on. Personal photographs and pictures from magazines can be titled and included. Memory wallets are small enough for participants to carry with them if they desire. These very popular items allow people to see familiar photographs, names, and information when they wish and can reduce anxiety for participants with mental impairments.

Materials: Notebooks, scrapbooks, or photo albums (full or pocket-sized); glue; magazines; photos

Movement to Music

Music as a motivator for physical exercise

Exercises are done to music of your selection or to videotapes such as Richard Simmons' popular *Sweatin' to the Oldies* series. Warm ups and cool downs are done to slow music, with a peppier beat between the two for more vigorous workouts.

Materials: Music and/or videos

Mural Painting

Self-expression on a large scale
Appropriate for cooperative groups or independent workers
Encourages group decision making and interaction

Create wall murals by painting on mural-sized paper from a craft store or large rolls of shelf or meat paper. For solo work, each artist paints an 11-by-17–inch picture, with the completed works being connected to make a larger picture. Groups can work together on each section of the mural.

One type of mural can be done by duplicating the same scene on four sheets of paper. The artists work together or individually to paint a representation of each of the four seasons. The group should strive for consistency throughout. For example, a roof which is painted red in the first scene should also be red in the other three. Other possible subjects for murals could include a landscape, ocean scene, jungle, or circus.

Materials: Paper, poster paint, markers, brushes, sponge applicators

Music Bingo

A musical twist on traditional bingo
Often results in a spontaneous sing-along
Song titles take the place of numbers on these bingo cards which are distributed to each player. Portions of songs are played, and participants mark off the songs that appear on their card. First player to complete a line of songs wins—just like in regular bingo.

To make the game, use 8-by-10–inch posterboard divided into squares, with a song title in each square. Songs can be taped or played on a piano or other instrument. Use a mix of 30s, 40s and 50s, traditional songs, and maybe an occasional contemporary surprise.

Materials: Music, musical bingo cards and markers, prizes, if desired, a purchased version is available from:

Third Age Press (Division of Amerson Ltd.)
PO Box 1200
Mattituck, NY 11952

Mystery Bag

Choose items around a theme to stimulate discussion
Fun for guessers and watchers alike
Fill a pillowcase with common items. Players feel the bag and try to identify objects. Items may be randomly chosen or may all relate to a theme, such as kitchen tools or things in a lady's purse.

Materials: Pillowcase, objects

Name That Artist

A favorite of music lovers
A perfect trigger for memories and reminiscence
Players try to identify the names of songs and/or the artist singing after hearing a short excerpt of the piece. This activity takes almost no preparation, but is always a hit. If no one can identify the song or artist, hints can be given.

Materials: Music

Nation or State Day

Honors your participants' roots
A perfect opportunity to try new experiences
A country or state is chosen as the theme of this day's activities. Decor can include travel posters of the area, reproductions of the flag, appropriate music, and the national anthem or state song can be played. An overview of the featured location can include historical highlights, chief products, customs, and

so on. Participants from this country or area can be spotlighted and invited to share their memories. Foods that represent the area may be served, although it is usually better to serve unfamiliar foods in small portions for tasting, rather than as an entire meal. Staff and/or participants can dress in costume or the colors of the nation's flag.

Travel agencies and libraries are good resources for this day. Staff, volunteers, participants, and their families may also have information on places they have visited. Ethnic organizations and churches may be able to provide speakers or entertainment.

Materials: Decorations, music, foods, resources, posters

National Christmas Trees

A unique holiday celebration
Recognizes cultural diversity

This project requires at least six weeks of research and planning, but can yield spectacular results. Donated or purchased trees are decorated in the tradition of different countries and cultures.

Materials: Trees, decorations will vary with country or culture chosen

Ninety-Plus Celebration

A salute to everyone who has passed this milestone
A great time to invite family and community
Especially appropriate during "Older Americans Week"

Participants age 90 and older and/or family members are asked to bring in photos for display. Photos can also be made into slides for a presentation. Relatives and friends write about each honoree, and tributes are made into a booklet. Each honoree is given a corsage and is interviewed about his or her life. Music spanning the years can be played; news highlights reviewed; and fads, fashions, and hairstyles recalled.

Materials: Photos, slides with projector, notebooks, corsages, music, refreshments

Oktoberfest

A traditional autumn festival
Celebrates German heritage

Participants and families of German descent or a local German association can help to plan an authentic Oktoberfest. Decorations, costumes, and music will create the atmosphere. If possible, arrange for a polka band to provide entertainment. Serve appropriate refreshments such as sausage, sauerkraut, German potato salad, brown bread, and potato pancakes. Beer is nearly always a part of Oktoberfests but can be one of the nonalcoholic variety. For a really special event, invite the community to join in your celebration.

Materials: Decorations, refreshments, music

Old Time Radio

A reminder of the pretelevision days

Participants listen to recordings of old radio shows. Afterward, they can share memories of favorite shows, characters, commercials, and radio performers.

Materials: Recordings of radio shows, tape player (tape prices start around $7.95). Available in larger audio stores or from:

Sea Bay Game Company
77 Cliffwood Avenue, Suite 1D
Cliffwood, NJ 07721
Phone (800) 568-0188
Fax (908) 583-7284
http://www.seabaygame.com

Parachute Games and Dance

A onetime purchase you'll use again and again
Works outdoors or indoors, seated or standing, for any number of players

A parachute is a must for your activity program! Participants sit or stand in a circle around the parachute, and each one holds on as the parachute is lowered and raised. A balloon or ball can be placed in the parachute, and music can be used to help direct movement. This is a great way to keep participants active, but they need to be monitored for signs of fatigue. The variations on parachute games are endless. One is to play a popular song and raise the parachute when a word starting with a particular letter is sung.

Materials: Parachute, foam ball or balloon, music; parachute prices range from $25 to $250 depending on size and features. Available from:

World Wide Games
P.O. Box 517
Colchester, CT 06415
Phone (800) 243-9232

Participant Volunteers

Gives purpose to your participants' days while filling volunteer positions for your facility
Increases self-esteem and feeling of usefulness

A volunteer program can be a perfect way for some of your participants to remain active and useful. Jobs must be tailored to the individual needs of each person, but a position can probably be found for anyone who wants one.

Participant volunteers should be treated with the same respect as other volunteers. They should be trained, their opinions should be heard, and their efforts should be recognized. Your participant volunteer positions will vary according to your participants' interests and abilities and your facility's needs. Possible positions for participant volunteers include

1. Office work—stapling, stuffing envelopes

2. Reception—greeters for your center, speakers or host/hostess for special events

3. Messenger—delivering mail or messages through facility, posting items on bulletin boards

4. Housekeeping—watering plants, dusting, folding laundry

5. Community volunteers—for example, delivering Meals on Wheels

6. Kitchen help—setting the table, washing dishes, shucking corn

7. Maintenance—light repairs in your facility

8. Yard work and gardening

9. Food preparation—cooking and baking, baking for bake sales and special events, preparing meals for ill community members

10. Crafts—making useful items for children's groups or other community members, creating crafts to be sold or given as gifts

11. Cards—writing birthday or get-well cards for participants and community members, writing thank-you cards to program presenters and volunteers

Penny Ante

Appropriate for a wide variety of functional levels
Encourages interaction among players
Each player is given a certain number of pennies. Players take turns drawing question cards and answering questions or following instructions. For example, a card might read, "Give a penny to each person who is a grandmother."
Materials: Pennies, game cards (approximately $14.95). Available from:

Sea Bay Game Company
77 Cliffwood Avenue, Suite 1D
Cliffwood, NJ 07721
Phone (800) 568-0188
Fax (732) 583-7284
http://www.seabaygame.com

Briggs Corporation
P.O. Box 1698
Des Moines, IA 50309–1698
Phone (877) 307-1744
Fax (800) 222-1996
http://www.briggscorp.com

Pen Pals/Voice Pals

Encourages interaction with a variety of people
Stimulates communication skills

Arrange for "pals" for your interested participants who can correspond by letter (written, typed, or dictated), audiotapes, or videotapes. Teachers are often happy to give their students practice in letter writing by becoming pen pals. Other sources to try include Scout troops, youth groups, church groups, other senior facilities, friends or relatives in other areas, and so on.

Materials: Stationery, pens, stamps; tapes and recorders for video or audio correspondence

Pet-Assisted Therapy/Petting Zoo

A source of pleasure, memories, and new experiences
A favorite program, appropriate for all functional levels and group sizes

The benefits of pet-assisted therapy have been well-documented and can be brought to your facility relatively easily. Even-tempered pets can be brought in by staff, family members, volunteers, 4H groups, or animal shelters.

Familiar animals like dogs and cats will remind participants of beloved pets. Farm animals will bring back memories from childhood for some, while exotic pets such as potbellied pigs or miniature hedgehogs can elicit surprise, laughter, and unexpected responses. (Check in advance for animal allergies among your participants.) Pets brought regularly will become favorites, while an occasional newcomer will keep interest level high.

A petting zoo or exhibit from a local farm or zoo can also be arranged and will be especially popular if the animals can be bottle or hand fed. (A commercial petting zoo can cost $150 or more.) Baby ducks in a pan of water are a portable favorite.

Materials: Animals

Photo Gallery

An opportunity to display treasured photographs
Great fun when done as a guessing game

Collect photographs from your participants and their families, as well as from staff and volunteers. Display these as a gallery in your center. Include childhood photos, wedding portraits, pictures of children, and so on. Many people are delighted to have the chance to "show off" how they looked as a bride or groom, at their graduation, or with their new baby.

A display of baby pictures is always popular, especially when combined with a "Guess the Picture?" contest where players try to identify the faces in the photos.

Materials: Photos

Pinecone Bird Feeders

Appropriate for a range of functional levels
Attracts feathered friends to be enjoyed by all

Large pinecones with a string attached to the top are filled with peanut butter, then rolled in bird seed. The feeders can be hung by a paper clip or hook and should be placed near a window for daily viewing.

Materials: Large pinecones, peanut butter, spoon or butter knife, bird seed, string, hooks or paper clips

Pizza Party

A favorite group cooking project

Prepare pizza crusts ahead. Each group of participants gets a crust which they top with sauce. The group chooses from a variety of toppings, then adds cheese. Bake at 400°F for about 12 minutes, cool, and enjoy a pizza party.

Materials: Pizza crusts, sauce, cheese, toppings (try to offer a variety, possibly including some more unusual choices like pineapple or broccoli), cooking utensils

Pocketball

A new twist on the old-fashioned skeeball game
A very popular activity with both men and women

This game requires a 36-by-36–inch board with a hole in each corner and one in the center. The holes should be big enough for a tennis ball to rest in, but not to fall through. (Board size can vary to fit your tables.) The front of the board rests on the table, with the back elevated 8 to 10 inches. Posterboard may be used to cover the opening between the board and table as needed. Players take turns rolling a set number of tennis balls. Corner holes "score" one point each, while the center is worth three points. Play continues for as many "frames" as you choose. If this game is played regularly, you can keep records of scores and hold an awards night where certificates or prizes are given for highest score, high average, and so on.

Materials: Plywood and tools to build board, blocks to elevate end of board, posterboard, tennis balls

Poetry Corner

For poets and poetry lovers alike
Can be adapted to a wide variety of occasions and topics

Many types of poetry lend themselves to this read-aloud activity—seasonal, spiritual, limericks, humor. Some participants may want to try their hand at writing original poetry and sharing it with the group.

Materials: Poetry

The Price Is Right

Our popular variation of the TV favorite
Stimulates a range of cognitive skills

Pictures of objects are taken from catalogs and magazines, with prices known only to the "master of ceremonies." The emcee describes each object up for bid, and four contestants who have been chosen in advance bid on the price. The contestant who comes closest without going over is awarded one point. The highest point total wins a prize at the end of the game.

A variation can be played with "yesterday's" prices, taken from a real or reprinted catalog from earlier years.

Materials: Pictures of items, prizes.

Rag Wreaths

Participants at a variety of levels will succeed
Can be made to fit any occasion and used for decorations, gifts, or fundraising

Fabric is cut with pinking shears into squares of about 4-by-4–inches. A screwdriver is used to force the center of each square into a straw wreath covered with cellophane or plastic wrap. Squares are closely placed to cover the entire front of the wreath. A bow or ribbon can be attached to finish the project.

Materials: Straw wreath covered with cellophane or wrapped in plastic wrap, pinking shears, fabric, screwdriver, ribbon

Reminiscence Discussions

Brings back fond memories
Unlimited variations possible

Each discussion focuses on a particular topic, with visual aids to spark conversation. Some of our favorites include the following:

1. Old-time candy samples like candy cigarettes, spearmint leaves, orange peanuts

2. Wildflowers such as violets, black-eyed Susans, bluebells

3. Old-fashioned cars—Show toy cars or models, pictures of older cars

4. Old-fashioned household items like rug beater, bed warmer, chamber pot, butter churn

5. School days reminders such as rulers, and fountain pens. Encourage participants to share poems and stories learned in school.

6. Old clothing and jewelry

7. Old magazines

8. Old toys

9. *Then and Now* books (Thunder Bay Press; check local bookstore or amazon.com) or newspaper columns. Libraries and historical societies can often supply pictures showing familiar locations as they have looked over the years.

Materials: Objects to be shown

Ring Toss Trivia

Combines physical and mental skills
"Right" answers earn rewards, but no one is left out
This variation on the popular ring toss game involves two teams which take turns at answering questions. Everyone gets at least one chance for a ringer, and a right answer earns an extra "toss."

Materials: Ring toss game, trivia questions. Ring toss and trivia available at larger toy and game stores. Eldertrivia (Volumes 1–6, about $10/set; also available in book form) also available from Flaghouse. Ring toss also available from World Wide Games:

FlagHouse
601 FlagHouse Drive
Hasbrouck Heights, NJ 07604
Phone (800) 793-7900
Fax (800) 793-7922
FlagHouse.com

World Wide Games
P.O. Box 517
Colchester, CT 06415
Phone (800) 243-9232

ROM Dance

Gentle exercise
Appropriate for a variety of physical levels
The ROM (Range of Music) Exercise and Relaxation Program includes a flowing progression of dance-like movements combined with meditation.

Materials: ROM kit including text, videotapes, and audiotapes $129.95. Available from:

ROM Institute
3601 Memorial Drive
Madison, WI 53704
Phone (800) 488-4940

Sensory Surprises

Puzzles to stimulate the senses

These activities are designed to awaken the senses and enhance discrimination. Costs are minimal, and materials can be varied according to availability and preparation time.

Visual Activities

Colors. Give each participant a swatch of material or piece of paper of a different color. Ask them to name or point out things which are the same color. A variation is to have the group take turns naming things until they run out of ideas, then move to another color.

Another color-related activity is "I see, I see," in which a player silently chooses an object, then says, for example, "I see, I see something that is blue." The group then asks yes and no questions and makes guesses until the object is identified.

Shapes. Participants are given shape cards (e.g., circle, triangle, diamond) and asked to identify as many objects as possible with that shape. This may also be played as a group, with each player taking a turn at naming an object.

Auditory Activities

Play recordings of commonly heard sounds (e.g., alarm clock, car horn, train whistle) and ask group members to identify the sounds. Recordings of group members' voices or very famous voices can provide an entertaining variation. Identifying famous singers or parts of songs is also a favorite.

Olfactory Activities

Provide a variety of distinctive scents and ask participants to identify as many as they can. Smells like pine, chocolate, vanilla, cinnamon, and lemon can be pleasing, and may encourage reminiscence and discussion. A variation would be to use scents related in some way. For example, a woodland activity might include flowers and plants. A variety of spices or fruits could be used for another activity.

Tactile Activities

Have participants feel and identify a variety of textures such as sandpaper, satin, tree bark, and cotton balls. (See also *Mystery Bag*.)

Tasting Activities

Give participants a taste of various foods to see if they can identify them without looking. Have them try to distinguish an apple from a pear, for example, or one type of apple from another. (See also *Taste Test*.)

Silhouettes

A great President's Day decoration
Participants sit between a projector and a piece of poster
board or heavy white paper. Their profiles are outlined with
pencil, then painted with black tempera paint. Outlines can
also be cut from black paper and attached to a white background. Display these "famous" silhouettes in your facility.
Materials: Projector or other bright light, posterboard/white paper, black
paint/black paper, pencil/chalk, glue/tape

Sing-Alongs

Include old standards, hymns, ethnic favorites—something for everyone
A favorite activity that involves little preparation or cost, but much enjoyment
Few will be able to resist joining in when they hear their favorite songs.
All you really need is music and a leader to get things started. Music can be
provided by a musician or from tapes or records. Sing-along records such as
those by Mitch Miller can also be bought or borrowed.
Materials: Music

SMILE (So Much Improvement With a Little Exercise)

Low-intensity workout appropriate for almost anyone
No special equipment needed
SMILE is designed for both active and inactive older adults, including
those with limited mobility. The program includes 41 chair-based or standing
exercises which can help to maintain or regain physical abilities.
Materials: SMILE manual and video. Although out-of-print, it is well
worth trying to find a copy for your program.

Snow Party

Brings the great outdoors indoors
Lightens up a gray wintry day
When everyone is sick of winter, use this theme day to celebrate the
snow. Bring the snow inside to an open area and have mini snowball fights,
or build tabletop snowmen. Other activities could include balloon volleyball
with white balloons or several balloons in a white garbage bag; making bird
feeders or snowmen decorations; playing a word game naming things that
have to do with snow. Refreshments can include snow-capped candies on a
"snowball" of vanilla ice cream.
Materials: White balloons, bag, craft materials, refreshments

Spiritual Activities

Recognize an important part of life for many of your participants
Offer comfort and increase coping skills

A continuation of familiar spiritual activities provides a source of support and strength for your participants and forges an important link between past and present. Nowhere is knowing your participants more important than in the area of spirituality. You must be very familiar with your participants' religious beliefs and backgrounds and will need the assistance of a religious leader or family member to plan a program.

Spiritual and religious activities are a sensitive subject, and the temptation may be to eliminate them rather than risk offense. However, these beliefs are such an integral part of a person that a truly participant-centered program cannot ignore them. Suggestions on creating spiritual programs for your participants include the following:

- Talk to the participant's family and friends. Find out as much as you can about his or her background and past practices. Enlist help in creating a program for your facility.

- Invite spiritual leaders to visit your facility.

- Observe religious holidays for all of your participants. Family and religious leaders can help if you are unfamiliar with observances.

- Make appropriate religious texts available and have staff or volunteers read to participants if they desire.

- Familiar prayers and songs can be comforting. Be familiar with some appropriate pieces for each participant and make adaptations for functional levels as needed.

- Offer a combination of one-on-one and group activities. Some participants may enjoy attending a service or observance associated with a different religion but should *never* feel pressured to do so.

Sports Fans' Favorites

Keep the sports lover's interest
Maintain physical activity level

While taking part in some sports activities may no longer be possible for your participants, a variety of games and modified sports should be available to encourage physical activity. A wide selection of games and sports equipment is available in most larger toy or sports stores and many can be used indoors or outdoors.

Some that we would recommend include

1. Automatic golf putt retriever

2. Mini golf set

3. Lawn bowling or indoor bowling set

4. Croquet

5. Rubber horseshoes

6. Remote control cars

7. Catch game (Velcro paddles or gloves with ball)

8. Shuffleboard

Squirt Gun Art

A chance to try "abstract art"
Lots of fun—no talent required

Squirt guns are filled with thinned tempera paint. Protect the area with plastic and hang up a sheet of paper. Artists take turns shooting at the paper to create an abstract masterpiece. This is a good outdoor project but may be done indoors if the walls and floor are covered.

Materials: Squirt guns, paint, paper, plastic sheets

Student Art Contest

Brings the community into your center
Ideal intergenerational activity

Arrange with a local school to display student art in your facility. You may want to include categories such as People and Families, Animals and Nature, and Holidays, as well as a "Free Expression" division. Participants judge the posters, and parents, children, community members, and media can be invited for an awards ceremony.

Materials: Ribbons and/or prizes

Tai Chi

Gentle exercise and relaxation

Tai chi exercises originated in China many years ago. Smooth, fluid movements are designed to stimulate muscles, joints, and internal organs without stress or strain and may be done in a seated position. It is advisable that a nurse or other medical professional lead the group and/or monitor participants. A number of tai chi videos are available for seniors. Check your local library or look online.

Materials: Tai chi videotape

Taste Test

A teaser for the discriminating palate

Participants take part in "blind" taste tests and try to identify similar products. For example, three cola products could be tested, with tasters trying to identify the products correctly, and choosing their favorites.

Materials: Three test products

They're Off!

A board game version of a day at the races

This purchased game involves rolling dice and advancing "horses" until a winner crosses the finish line.

Materials: *They're Off* horse racing game (includes 5½-foot felt track, 5-inch plastic horses, dice, and a deck of numbered cards. Under $30 for basic game; about $80 for deluxe version. Available from:

    Sea Bay Game Company
    77 Cliffwood Avenue, Suite 1D
    Cliffwood, NJ 07721
    Phone (800) 568-0188
    Fax (732) 583-7284
    http://www.seabaygame.com

This Is Your Life

A variation on the classic television program
Recognizes the uniqueness of everyone's life

This program highlights one participant at a time and should be held on a regular basis, such as once a month. Information and photographs of the featured person are collected in advance. They are then displayed and shared with the group. Family members and friends should also be included in the celebration when possible. A keepsake book is created to be given to the honoree.

Materials: Keepsake book, photographs

Toss Across

A combination bean bag toss/tic-tac-toe game

Players or teams try to score three in a row by tossing bean bags onto a game board

Materials: *Toss Across* game (available in toy or discount stores)

Treasured Memories

Taps forgotten memories
Helps your participants get to know one another
In this game, players move around a board and pick up question cards. Typical cards might include questions such as, "Did you move often as a child?" or may request an action such as "Sing your favorite childhood song."
Materials: *Treasured Memories* game (about $25). Available from:
Sea Bay Game Company
77 Cliffwood Avenue, Suite 1D
Cliffwood, NJ 07721
Phone (800) 568-0188
Fax (732) 583-7284
http://www.seabaygame.com

Un-Holiday Celebrations

Makes any day a holiday
Sometimes you just need a holiday. If there's no "real" celebration lurking on the horizon—invent one! Every day of the year has been designated as the day to honor *something* and, with a little imagination, can be turned into a theme day or party.
One nursing home went all out for National Pig Day on March 1. They arranged for a local potbellied pig club to bring their pets on that day and sent press releases and invitations to residents' families. On March 1, the facility was decorated, and staff members wore pig noses. The pigs performed a show and visited with the audience. Of course, everyone was given the chance to "pig out" on refreshments after the show.
Your celebrations can be elaborate or simple. Maybe Elvis Presley's birthday (January 8) is the time to play some of "The King's" music. National Juggling Day (June 17) is the perfect occasion to bring in a juggler or to let staff and participants try their hand.
In the Appendix we've reproduced a listing of special days. Other lists are probably available at your library. You may also want to make up your own holidays to commemorate special people and features of your facility. Materials and costs will vary widely, but the therapeutic value will include enjoyment.

Veterans' Tribute

An honor for all veterans
Especially appropriate for Veterans' Day or Memorial Day
For this salute, interview each veteran in your facility, and post his or her contributions on an honor board and/or in your newsletter. Ask a veteran from the local American Legion or other veterans' group to speak at your ceremony.

Family members of each veteran should also be invited. Each veteran should be honored individually, and small flags or other gifts may be presented. Patriotic music and refreshments put the finishing touches on your tribute.

Materials: Flags or gifts, music, refreshments

Wading Pool

A just-for-fun activity for steamy summer days
Waders kick off their shoes and wade or dangle their feet into a pool of water
Materials: Plastic wading pool with water, chairs

Walkers' Club

Gradually increases activity with visible measures of progress
Beneficial for those recently discharged from rehabilitation programs
A walking route is designed with a marker (e.g., paper or chalk footprints) placed every ten feet. Daily progress is recorded on a chart. After a designated time period, a certificate is presented to each walker in recognition of his or her mileage. Categories for walkers may be created according to their levels. For example, pacers might walk 20 feet a day, but striders would walk 100 feet.

Materials: Certificates, notebook for recordkeeping, chalk/paper feet

Wall of Fame

A place to display triumphs, large or small
Choose a large wall or bulletin board at a central location in your facility. Participants, staff, and volunteers are invited to brag about their accomplishments and those of their families and friends. Include photos of grandchildren, newspaper clippings, certificates, awards and anything else that is a source of pride for someone in your facility. A "Remember When" section offers the opportunity to display past triumphs.

Materials: Bulletin board

Welcome Luncheon

Helps newcomers feel at home
Monthly luncheons or teas can be held to welcome participants, volunteers, or staff new to your program. Staff members and veteran participants can act as hosts and hostesses for this special lunch or tea. Information about your facility and its programs can be presented. Newcomers should also be given the opportunity to ask questions and to talk about themselves if they wish.

Materials: Refreshments

Who Am I?

Introduces each participant in a new light
Recognizes the importance of past accomplishments

Information on each participant is gathered in advance. The group leader describes a person to the group without revealing his or her identity. A few details such as birthplace and siblings are given, followed by more information such as maiden name, career, or number of children until the identity is guessed.

Wisdom of Confucious

An opportunity to learn about the Chinese culture

This day is devoted to learning about the teachings and sayings of Confucious. Appropriate foods may be served—with chopsticks, of course—ending the meal with a fortune cookie. Chinese New Year's offers a perfect opportunity for this celebration.

Materials: Book on Confucious, food related to Chinese culture

Chapter 6
The Best Medicine:
Incorporating Humor Into Your Program

You don't stop laughing because you grow old,
you grow old because you stop laughing.
                                        —Michael Pritchard

We can all name the things we lose as we age—muscle tone, sensory acuity, and even a bit of our height. Fortunately, our sense of humor isn't on the list. What a wonderful gift it is that we can continue to laugh throughout our lives!

In our Center, we're reminded again and again that humor is a part of life at any age. Not long ago, one of the women in our adult day center struck up a conversation with a young gentleman visitor. A staff member tried to ask a question, but was cut short when our participant smiled mischievously and said, "Don't bother me now—I'm talking to a man!"

Why Humor?

What if you heard about a miracle treatment that stimulates muscles, improves circulation, strengthens the heart, helps with clot prevention, aids digestion, boosts the immune system, and more? You would probably think that it sounded too good to be true, but the truth is that this "wonder drug" is free and readily available to all. It's called laughter.

In 1964, Norman Cousins, editor of the *Saturday Review,* was diagnosed with a chronic degenerative disease and was offered almost no hope for recovery. Facing a painful future, Cousins decided to test his belief that a positive attitude and sense of humor could have dramatic effects on physical conditions. With the consent of his doctor, Cousins left his hospital bed and checked into a hotel, where he filled his days with humor. He watched comedy movies and videos of his favorite comedians and visited with supportive friends. The impact on Cousins' disease was so dramatic—overcoming a crippling form of arthritis—that he was later asked to be a lecturer on humor therapy for the UCLA medical staff.

Physiological benefits of humor involve nearly all of the major systems of our bodies. Laughter stimulates muscles and improves circulation. The increased respiratory rate means more oxygen for the body. Some experts believe that the immune system is boosted as a result of stimulation of the thymus and a rise in immunoglobulin A. Laughter also stimulates the pituitary gland, causing a release of endorphins and enkeflins, the body's natural pain killers.

Laughter can also significantly affect cognitive and psychological function. Increases in adrenaline and endorphins can boost alertness and memory and enhance creativity and learning. Humor can encourage problem solving, give perspective, help with coping, increase motivation and morale, prevent burnout, enhance self-esteem, improve communication, and develop relationships. Wow! Also, according to Dr. Joel Goodman, stress-related hormones appear to be suppressed through laughter. As Dr. Goodman says, "…although stress may be inevitable in life, the negative physiological toll…doesn't have to be there."

Guidelines for Using Humor Effectively

Laughter is the shortest distance between two people.
—Victor Borge

Use good taste and common sense in choosing your materials. It's usually best to avoid off-color jokes and language and "hot button" subjects like ethnicity, sex, religion, and politics. When in doubt, leave it out.

Be sure to laugh with others, not at them. Some people love a joke at their own expense; others definitely do not. Be sensitive to your participants' feelings, and never make light of something important to them.

Tune in to your audience. Choose topics to which they will be able to relate. Jokes about current fads and personalities, however funny, will fall flat if they are unfamiliar to your group.

Use sarcasm and irony rarely if at all. Participants, especially those with functional impairments, may be confused or hurt, or may take everything you say literally.

Don't feel that you have to be a comedian—although it couldn't hurt! You don't have to be funny to have fun. Take advantage of the naturally funny people around you—participants, staff, volunteers, and guests—and get them involved. Don't expect everyone to participate. Some are born to be in the limelight, while others are most comfortable as observers.

Keep your format loosely structured and relaxed. Some of our best times have occurred when we just went with the flow. For example, once during hand exercises with rubber balls, one of the participants began to lightly pummel the group leader with the ball. The rest of the group followed suit, and they were soon collapsed in laughter. Another time our official "garden waterer" decided to water our activities coordinator instead. She could have been stuffy and classified this as "inappropriate behavior." Instead, she appreciated the humor and was delighted that our participant felt comfortable enough in our Center to play a joke on her.

Encourage the participants to suggest programs and to give feedback on what they enjoy. Give each participant a chance to display his or her unique sense of humor. One woman in our Center entertains us constantly with her point of view. When asked how she is, she will invariably reply, "Fine as a frog's hair split in two, and that's pretty fine." She also regularly recites a poem for our staff members which begins, "Twas the night before payday…"

Use humor with your staff and volunteers. They need the stress-reduction and a morale boost, too, and it will give the participants the chance to see "the professionals" in a new light.

Know your participants. (You didn't really think we could resist saying it again, did you?) You may have a participant who loves a racy joke or thrives on a good political jab. Throw the rule book out the window, and tailor your one-on-one humor to fit this person.

Humor Activities

Laughter is a vaccine for the ills of the world.
—Joey Adams

Film Funnies

If humor therapy is new to your program, people may be hesitant to join in. Some carefully selected videos will get your first group started or serve as a warm-up for any session. By experimenting with a variety of comedy styles, you are bound to find a way to tickle even the most reluctant funny bone. Red Skelton, Jack Benny, Bob Hope, Abbott and Costello, Victor Borge, and the "blooper" videos are just a sampling of material available.

Can You Kazoo?

Pass out kazoos to everyone in the room and let the music begin. When your band is ready, perform for an audience and share the fun.

The Good Old Summertime

Indulge yourselves on a warm day with some favorites from childhood. Watermelon seed spitting contests, ice cream making, hula hoop competitions, and bubble blowing can bring out the kid in everyone.

Most Embarrassing Moment

We've all had them. Invite group members to lead the fun by sharing a humorous past disaster. We've learned that participants particularly appreciate jokes at the staff's expense.

> After one of our directors sat on a wet car seat, she ended up with a large and obvious spot on her pants. It was a busy day, so she proceeded to work at her computer—with a hair dryer stuck down her pants to solve her dilemma. It would have worked fine if she hadn't been "caught." Participants and staff alike enjoyed the sight and hurried to share the story, but no one laughed harder than the director herself.

Share a Joke Day

There's a little Milton Berle in everyone, so encourage each participant to bring a favorite joke to the group. Record the real side-splitters for future retellings.

Juggling Day

Look for books, videos (we use one by Steve Allen, Jr.), and the "Juggling for Klutzes" kits to get things going. A few coordinated individuals may actually learn to juggle, but the rest will provide the humor.

Laugh Tracks

Everyone has a unique laugh, and some are downright contagious. Record people from your group and play "Name that Laugh." Just playing a recording of a really infectious laugh will start a chain reaction. We also leave our doors open during humor activities. The sound of laughter never fails to draw people in as their curiosity over "what's so funny" gets the best of them.

The Play's the Thing

Skits can be equally entertaining for actors and audience. One of our gentlemen, who has experienced a series of setbacks including heart surgery and a battle with cancer, showed off his sense of humor when he donned wedding duds to play the "bride" in our shotgun wedding skit. On another occasion, we invited one of our infrequent participants in the senior center to play the part of a Greek god, complete with robe and crown of leaves. He performed admirably and became one of our regulars. Our participants also love the skits put on by the staff in which we make fools of ourselves—the sillier the better.

Comedy Central

A bulletin board can serve as your humor center when decorated with jokes, puns, cartoons, quotes, stories, and pictures. Invite everyone in your facility to contribute their favorites. We also hang photos or magazine pictures and add captions or invite viewers to create their own. As items are changed, we save the old ones in a scrapbook for future enjoyment. We've mounted our bulletin boards in the restrooms to play to captive audiences. Cardboard "table tents" with jokes and one-liners will capture attention if placed in the dining room or other high traffic areas.

Comedy Carts and Humor Rooms

These stockpiles for humor "are wonderful ways to legitimize humor and make it more accessible" according to Dr. Goodman (The Humor Project). Include audios and videos, reading materials, games, posters, buttons, clown noses, and other gag items—anything for a laugh.

Even if laughter didn't offer all of the benefits we've listed, it would still be important just because it feels so good. It has a way of spreading from person to person and uniting them despite their differences. A shared laugh can remind us that we are all in this thing called life together and doing the best we can despite absurd odds.

A person without a sense of humor is like a wagon without springs, jolted by every pebble in the road.
—Henry Ward Beecher

Chapter 7
Are We There Yet?
Evaluating Your Activity Program

You've carefully selected the perfect activities for your participants and facility. The staff and volunteers have been trained and are comfortable with their roles. Your participant-centered activity program is in full swing. Now it's time to sit back and pat yourself on the back for a job well done, right? Well, yes—but only for a moment. Your work is far from done.

In fact, as you probably suspect, your work will never be done. An activity program isn't a finished product. It's an ongoing process that will need to be fine-tuned regularly and may even require a major overhaul once in a while. Your facility changes constantly, and a program that met your needs six months ago may not be appropriate today. Why? The foremost reason is that your participants change. New people come in, others leave. In addition, the functional changes associated with aging will cause the needs of individual participants to change, too. Add to that the inevitable changes in staff, volunteers, and budget, and you will understand why regular reassessment is a must. The success of your program depends on the success of your individual activities.

We hope that we may have given you some new ideas, but only your staff can decide what works in your facility. Each new activity should be assessed before it is added to the program. Even tried and true activities need to be reassessed on a regular basis to be sure that they are still working in your program. You must consider a number of factors in deciding whether an activity is right for your population, including the following:

- *Dignity*. Is this an appropriate adult activity? As stated in Chapter 1, activities cannot be childish or insulting. They can, however, be fun and encourage playfulness or silliness. You have to decide where to draw the line.

- *Meaningfulness*. Can the participants see a reason to take part in this activity? Busywork activities that are not enjoyable serve no purpose.

- *Autonomy*. Does the activity offer choices? The first choice, of course, is whether the participants wish to take part. Sometimes gentle encouragement and coaxing may be needed, but if people have to be pressured to take part, it is not an appropriate activity.

- *Relevance*. Is this activity meeting the goals of your care plans? While every activity cannot and need not meet a goal for every single person, most should help to accomplish this purpose. For example, a person with Alzheimer's disease may be able to enjoy crossword puzzles in the early stages of the disease, but will experience great frustration if expected to continue as the condition progresses. Be sure that your activities correspond to the current abilities of your participants.

- *Staff*. Do you have the staff or volunteers to run this activity properly? Will they have the needed training and preparation time to do a good job?

- *Benefits Versus Cost*. Is this activity offering enough benefit to your participants to justify its cost? When considering this question, don't forget to count staff hours used, including preparation time. Even if you are using volunteers, think about whether this is the most productive use of their time.

- *Results*. Is this activity accomplishing what you had hoped it would? In addition to achieving care plan goals, is it stimulating and enjoyable? Do participants willingly join in the activity or ask that it be repeated? If no one is deriving satisfaction from the activity, it doesn't belong in your program no matter how many goals it may accomplish on paper.

- *Variety*. Even a favorite activity can be overdone. Is this one still greeted with enthusiasm? If not, it may be time to put it on hiatus for a little while and try something new. You can always reintroduce the old favorite another time.

Yikes! More Paperwork!?!

Once an activity has been tried, an evaluation form should be filled out. A notebook or file of past successes and failures in your activity program can be a lifesaver for future staff and volunteers and save wear and tear on your memory. Otherwise, you may keep trying programs that have been tried previously without the benefit of what was learned the last time. We include a sample evaluation form (p. 80), but any format that works for your staff would be fine. The important thing is that you consistently keep records on your activities. Of course, numbers on attendance and so on will also be needed for regulatory reports.

In addition to the evaluation form, you may want to keep track of who your participants were and how well each individual responded to the activity. A clear success or failure might be noted in the participant's file for future reference. Try to get the reactions of any staff and volunteers present for the activity.

Don't forget to talk to the participants themselves about an activity. Encourage them to express both negative and positive feelings. Find out if they would willingly participate again. This information alone may influence your decision on whether this activity is a keeper.

Can This Activity Be Saved?

Sometimes it happens—an activity bombs. You think you did everything right. It should have worked, but it didn't. So where do you go from here? Do you try again hoping for better results? Can you make changes that will increase your chances for success? Do you cut your losses and drop this particular activity from your plans?

Your first inclination may be to scuttle the activity. That's okay. If it's truly a disaster, this may be your best bet. There are always other activity choices out there, and your next one may be a smashing success. If you're not quite ready to throw in the towel on this activity, however, you'll need to conduct a postmortem to figure out what went wrong and whether it can or should be fixed. Consider the following points:

- *Setting*. When and where did you hold the activity? A physical activity might work better early in the day when energy levels are high, whereas a quiet one might be a better choice for the afternoon. If your participants are usually restless after the weekend, don't plan challenging, new activities for Monday. Was the area large enough? Were there a lot of distractions from other areas? Talk to staff and participants to find out if they were comfortable and able to see and hear what was going on.

- *Participants*. Was the activity appropriate for the people who took part? Consider whether it might have been too far above or below

Activity Evaluation

Activity _____

Date/Time _____

Location _____

Participants _____ # Staff _____ # Volunteers _____

Description of activity _____

_____

_____

Materials needed _____

_____

Preparation time _____ Cost _____

Reaction of participants/staff _____

_____

_____

_____

Would you recommend that we repeat this activity? _____

Recommendations (e.g., improvements, adaptations, changes) _____

_____

_____

Completed by _____

the functional level of the participants. Also look at the makeup of the group. If the activity required a lot of verbal participation, a group of quiet or unresponsive people could spell disaster. Would adding a couple of talkers to the mix make a difference? Certain personalities don't work well together, and may require a restructuring of the group or more staff participation.

- *Staff.* Your group leader and other staff and volunteers can make or break an activity. The sing-along leader shouldn't be the self-conscious staffer who can't carry a tune. Replacing a shy leader with a more outgoing one can sometimes encourage group members to participate. Look for your staff's strengths and assign them accordingly.

- *Instruction.* How was the activity taught to the group? Was it explained in appropriate language and broken down into steps that the group could understand and follow? A clearer explanation and demonstration may be needed.

- *Materials.* Did the materials work as you expected? Did you have sufficient craft supplies or game pieces for all participants? If most of the time is spent waiting for a turn, the activity is unlikely to hold the participants' attention.

- *Success.* Did the participants experience success? If the majority were unable to participate in any meaningful way, the activity may not have been appropriate. Look for adaptations or variations that will increase their success rate. Did the activity itself work the way you expected? Sometimes an activity that sounds good on paper may not work in practice and may need some creative changes.

If you've considered all of these and the activity is still a loser, it's time to move on. We've all had our share of misfires and disasters. Keep your sense of humor, put it in perspective, and proceed to that next activity. It may just be the one.

Appendix A

Sample Schedule and Special Celebrations

Sample Schedule: DECEMBER

Monday	Tuesday	Wednesday	Thursday	Friday
1 10:00 Current Events 10:30 Parachute 11:00 Celebrate Dates 1:00 Reminiscence 2:00 They're Off 3:00 Snack	**2** 10:00 Current Events 10:30 Exercise 11:00 Days in December 1:00 Sing-along 2:30 Jeopardy 3:30 Armchair Traveler	**3** 10:00 Current Events 10:30 ROM Dance 11:00 Christmas Customs 1:00 Poetry 2:00 Games and Music 3:00 Snack	**4** 10:00 Current Events 10:30 Bible Study 11:00 Christmas Foods 1:00 Sing-along 2:30 Trivia 3:30 SMILE Program	**5** 10:00 Current Events 10:30 ROM Dance 11:00 Reminiscence 1:00 News and Views 2:00 Games and Music 3:00 Snack
8 10:00 Current Events 11:00 Trivia 12:30 Ball Toss 1:30 Personal Bio 2:00 Snack 2:30 Celebrate Dates	**9** 10:00 Current Events 11:00 Music and Games 12:30 ROM Dance 1:30 Reminiscence 2:00 Snack 2:30 Christmas Customs	**10** 10:00 Current Events 11:00 Trivia 12:30 SMILE Program 1:30 Armchair Traveler 2:00 Snack 2:30 Days in December	**11** 10:00 Current Events 11:00 Music and Games 12:30 Exercise 1:30 Word Games 2:00 Snack 2:30 Christmas Quiz	**12** 10:00 Current Events 11:00 Trivia 12:30 Exercise 1:30 News and Views 2:00 Snack 2:30 Christmas Words
15 10:00 Current Events 10:30 Parachute 11:30 Word Games 1:00 Bible Study 2:00 Reminiscence 2:30 Snack	**16** 10:00 Current Events 10:30 Exercise 11:30 Personal Bio 1:00 Christmas Trivia 2:00 Ball Toss 2:30 Snack	**17** 10:00 Current Events 10:30 Parachute 11:30 Crossword Puzzle 1:00 They're Off 2:00 Games 2:30 Snack	**18** 10:00 Current Events 10:30 Exercise 11:30 Music and Games 1:00 Baking 3:00 Ball Toss 3:30 Snack	**19** 10:00 Current Events 10:30 Parachute 11:30 World Christmas 1:00 Poetry 2:00 Personal Bio 2:30 Snack
22 10:00 Current Events 10:30 ROM Dance 11:30 News and Views 1:00 Jeopardy 2:00 World Christmas 3:00 Snack	**23** 10:00 Current Events 10:30 ROM Dance 11:30 Music and Games 1:00 Christmas Trivia 2:00 Celebrate Dates 3:00 Snack	**24** 10:00 Current Events 10:30 ROM Dance 11:30 Reminiscence 1:00 Sing-along 2:00 Christmas Words 3:00 Snack	**25** Center Closed Merry Christmas!	**26** 10:00 Current Events 10:30 ROM Dance 11:30 Poetry 1:00 Word Games 2:00 Bible Study 3:00 Snack
29 10:00 Current Events 10:30 Exercise 11:30 Poetry 12:30 Crossword Puzzle 1:30 Music and Games	**30** 10:00 Current Events 10:30 Parachute 11:30 They're Off 12:30 New Year's Trivia 1:30 News and Views	**31** 10:00 Current Events 10:30 SMILE Program 11:30 Armchair Traveler 12:30 Reminiscence 1:30 Personal Bio		

Celebrations for the Month of January

Monthly Celebrations

National Soup Month
National Prune Breakfast Month
National Hot Tea Month
National Eye Care Month
National Book Blitz Month
Stamp Collectors Month
National Oatmeal Month

Weekly Celebrations

Universal Letter Writing Week (1st week)
Someday We'll Laugh About This Week (2nd week)
Cuckoo Dancing Week (3rd week)
Junior Achievement Week (Final week)

Daily Celebrations

3rd Monday   Martin Luther King Jr.'s Birthday (observed)

3rd Saturday   Hot and Spicy Food International Day

1   New Year's Day

1   St. Basil's Day —observed by the Greek Orthodox Church; special traditions include serving St. Basil cakes, which each contain a coin

4   Trivia Day

5   George Washington Carver Day

5   Twelfth Night—last or 12th night of the Christmas season

6   Three King's Day or Epiphany

8   Battle of New Orleans Day

8   World Literacy Day

8   International Women's Day—in Greece men do the housework and look after the children while the women relax

8   Birthday of Elvis Presley (1935–1977)

9   Show-and-Tell Day at Work

11   National Thank-You Day

13   Blame Someone Else Day

14   Secret Pal Day

15   Birthday of Martin Luther King, Jr. (1929–1968)

15   Humanitarian Day

16   Religious Freedom Day

17   Birthday of Benjamin Franklin (1706–1790)

19   Confederate Heroes Day—honoring Robert E. Lee (1807–1870) and Jefferson Davis (1808–1889); also Robert E. Lee's birthday

21   National Hugging Day

23   Birthday of John Hancock (1737–1793) and National Handwriting Day—to encourage more legible handwriting

23   National Pie Day

27   National Backwards Day

28   Bald Eagle Day

28   National Kazoo Day

29   National Puzzle Day

31   Explorer I, first U.S. satellite, is launched (1958)

Celebrations for the Month of February

Monthly Celebrations

American History Month
National African American History Month
International Friendship Month
Potato Lovers' Month
National Crime Prevention Month
Heart Month
Canned Food Month
Great American Pies Month
International Embroidery Month
Wild Bird Feeding Month
National Cherry Month
National Fiber Focus Month
National Snack Food Month

Weekly Celebrations

National Kraut and Frankfurter Week (2nd week)
Celebration of Love Week (3rd week)
International Friendship Week (3rd week)
Homes for Birds Week (3rd week)
National Pancake Week (Final week)

Daily Celebrations

3rd Monday President's Day
    1 Be an Encourager Day
    1 Robinson Crusoe Day
    1 National Freedom Day—commemorates the ratification of the 13th Amendment to the U.S. Constitution by President Abraham Lincoln, abolishing slavery
    2 Groundhog Day
    4 United Service Organization founded (1941)
    5 Weatherman's Day
  10 Gold Rush Days
  11 National Inventors Day
  12 Birthday of Abraham Lincoln (1809–1865)
  12 World Marriage Day

13   Get a Different Name Day

14   Valentine's Day

14   National Have-a-Heart Day

15   Senior Day

15   Birthday of Susan B. Anthony (1820–1906)

15   *USS Maine* mysteriously blows up in the Havana Harbor (1898)

16   Cultural Diversity Day

20   Student Volunteer Day

22   Birthday of George Washington (1732–1799)

28   International Pancake Day

29   Leap Year Day or Bachelor's Day—additional day every fourth year to make up for time lost annually when the 365 ¼ day cycle is computed as 366

Celebrations for the Month of March

Monthly Celebrations

National Peanut Month
National Nutrition Month
Women's History Month
Red Cross Month
National Sauce Month
National Noodle Month
National Frozen Food Month
National Craft Month

Weekly Celebration

Return Borrowed Books Week (1st week)
American Camp Week (2nd week)
Girl Scout Week (2nd week)
National Aardvark Week (2nd week)
Save Your Vision Week (2nd week)
National Procrastination Week (2nd week)
Universal Women's Week (2nd week)
Employ the Older Worker Week (2nd week)
American Chocolate Week (3rd week)
National Wildlife Week (3rd week)
Art Week (Final week)

Daily Celebrations

Mardi Gras/Shrove Tuesday (Tuesday before Ash Wednesday)
Ash Wednesday marks the beginning of Lent, and generally occurs in March,
but may occur in late February.

1 National Pig Day

3 Dolls' festival, Hina Matsuri—an annual Japanese national festival to honor little girls and their dolls

3 National Anthem Day

3 I Want You to Be Happy Day

4 Constitution Day (1789)

10 Salvation Army arrives in the United States (1880)

10 Invention of the telephone (1876)

11 Johnny Appleseed Day

11　Birthday of Lawrence Welk (1903–1992)

12　Girl Scout Day

14　Moth Day—to honor moth collectors and specialists

16　Freedom of Information Day

16　Docking Day—anniversary of the first docking of one spaceship with another, accomplished by U.S. astronauts Neil Armstrong and David Scott (1966)

17　Saint Patrick's Day

17　Birthday of Nat "King" Cole (1919–1965)

19　Last episode of *The Mary Tyler Moore Show* airs (1970–1977)

20　National Agriculture Day—tribute to farmers, ranchers, and growers

21　Memory Day

21　Fragrance Day

22　National Goof Off Day

22　National Sing Out Day

26　"Make Up Your Own Holiday" Day

29　Vietnam Veterans' Day—withdrawal of American forces from Vietnam (1973)

29　Knights of Columbus Founder's Day (1882)

30　Doctor's Day (since 1842)—commemorating the first use of anesthetic during surgery by Dr. Crawford W. Long

31　Bunsen Burner Day

Celebrations for the Month of April

Monthly Celebrations

Boost Your Hometown Month
Red Cross Month
National Anxiety Month
International Guitar Month
Keep America Beautiful Month
Listening Awareness Month
National Humor Month
National Garden Month
National Knuckles Down Month (tradition of playing marbles)
National Woodworking Month

Weekly Celebrations

Straw Hat Week (1st week)
Passion Week (1st week)
Egg Salad Week (1st full week after Easter)
National Garden Week (2nd week)
Heritage Week (3rd week)
Keep America Beautiful Week (3rd week)
National Library Week (3rd week)
Reading is Fun Week (Final week)
Sky Awareness Week (Final week)
Need a Volunteer Week (Final week)
Canada-U.S. Goodwill Week (Final week)
Jewish Heritage Week (Final week)
Intergenerational Week (Final week)

Daily Celebrations

Passover, Palm Sunday, Holy Thursday (Thursday before Easter), Good Friday (Friday before Easter), and Easter generally occur in April, but may occur in late March

2nd Sunday   National Home Safety Week

4th Thursday   Take Your Daughters to Work Day

1   Sorry, Charlie Day—honor Charlie the Tuna; to honor those who've been rejected and lived through it

1   April Fools' Day

3   Armenian Appreciation Day

 7 National Arbor Day

10 Humane Day—American Society for the Prevention of Cruelty to Animals chartered (1866)

11 Barbershop Quartet Day

13 Birthday of Thomas Jefferson (1743–1826)

15 Rubber Eraser Day

18 Look-Alike Day

22 Earth Day

24 General Federation of Women's Clubs Day

24 Administrative Professionals Day (4th Wednesday)

26 Richter Scale Day

27 Babe Ruth Day

28 National Arbor Day

28 Great Poetry Reading Day

28 Kiss Your Mate Day

30 National Honesty Day

Celebrations for the Month of May

Monthly Celebrations

National Barbecue Month
Older Americans Month
Physical Fitness and Sports Month
Asian Pacific Heritage Month
National Salad Month
Better Sleep Month
National Bike Month
National Egg Month
National Hamburger Month
National Seniors Travel Month
National Strawberry Month
Revise Your Work Schedule Month

Weekly Celebrations

Be Kind to Animals Week (1st week)
National Pet Week (1st week)
Cartoon Art Appreciation Week (1st week)
National Postcard Week (2nd week)
National Herb Week (2nd week)
National Transportation Week (3rd week)
National Police Week (3rd week)
National Senior Smile Week (3rd week)
International Pickle Week (3rd week)
National Frozen Yogurt Week (Final week)

Daily Celebrations

1st Friday	May Fellowship Day—An opportunity to explore women's various roles
1st Friday	International Tuba Day
1st Saturday	Astronomy Day
2nd Sunday	Mother's Day
3rd Saturday	Armed Forces Day
Final Monday	Memorial Day
Final Wednesday	Senior Health and Fitness Day

1   Save the Rhino Day

1   May Day—traditionally a day of flower festivals; celebrated with hanging of May Baskets and dancing around May Poles in England and some sections of the United States

1   Law Day—established to enhance citizens' awareness of the benefits of law and order

2   Robert's Rules Day—Birthday of Henry M. Robert (1837–1923), author of *Roberts Rules of Order,* a standard parliamentary guide

3   Lumpy Rug Day—to honor those who sweep difficult issues under the rug

5   Cinco de Mayo—celebrating the victory of the Mexican army over the French at Battalla de Pueblo (1862)

7   *RMS Lusitania* sunk by a German U-boat off the coast of Ireland (1915)

8   No Socks Day—Give up wearing socks for one day; it will mean less laundry, and you will feel a bit freer

8   V-E Day—end of WWII (1945)

12 National Hospital Day—birthday of Florence Nightingale (1820–1910)

15 Nylon stockings invented (1939)

16 Biographers Day—recommended to start reading or writing biographies

17 World Communications Day

18 Visit Your Relatives Day

18 Birthday of Whistler's Mother—celebrate sound of whistling

22 National Maritime Day—*USS Savanah* sets sail on the first steam-powered transatlantic voyage from Savannah, GA

25 National Tap Dance Day

29 Birthday of John F. Kennedy (1917–1963)

31 Anniversary of Johnstown Flood (1889)

Celebrations for the Month of June

Monthly Celebrations

National Dairy Month
National Ragweed Month
American Rivers Month
Turkey Lovers Month
National Rose Month
National Iced Tea Month
National Frozen Yogurt Month
National Fresh Fruit and Vegetable Month

Weekly Celebrations

International Volunteers Week (1st week)
National Safe Boating Week (1st week)
Pet Appreciation Week (2nd week)
National Little League Week (2nd week)
National Flag Week (2nd week)
National Clay Week (3rd week)

Daily Celebrations

Shavout (Jewish holy day) usually occurs in June

3rd Sunday Father's Day

1   Donut Day

3   Repeat Day—try to learn a new word by repeating it

4   National Frozen Yogurt Day

6   Philatelic Journalists' Day

7   Boone Day—Daniel Boone (1734–1820) first sighted land that would be Kentucky

8   Birthday of Frank Lloyd Wright (d. 1959)

9   Seniors' Day

10 Birthday of Judy Garland (1922–1969)

10 National Yo-Yo Day

11 Race Unity Day—to promote racial harmony and understanding

12 National Baseball Hall of Fame opens (1939)

14 Family History Day

14 Flag Day (1777)

16 United Cerebral Palsy's Casual Day—dress casual for the day

17 Watergate Day

17 National Juggling Day

17 Bunker Hill Day

18 International Picnic Day

19 Birthday of cartoon cat Garfield (1978)

21 Summer solstice (1st day of summer)

24 National Forgiveness Day

25 Log Cabin Day

28 National Columnist's Day

28 Anniversary of beginning and ending of WWI (1914–1919)

Celebrations for the Month of July

Monthly Celebrations

Anti-Boredom Month
National Recreation and Parks Month
National July Belongs to Blueberries Month
National Ice Cream Month
National Tennis Month
Eye Safety Month
National Hot Dog Month
National Baked Bean Month

Weekly Celebrations

Be Nice to New Jersey Week (1st week)
Freedom Week (2nd week)
Special Recreation Week (2nd week)

Daily Celebrations

4th Saturday Children's Day

1 Half-Year Day—public holiday in Hong Kong providing a mid-year day of relaxation for all citizens

1 American Stamp Day—anniversary of the issuance of the first U.S. postage stamps (1847)

2 Date that marks the halfway point of the year—at noon, 182 $\frac{1}{2}$ days have passed and 182 $\frac{1}{2}$ remain

3 Stay Out of the Sun Day—give your skin a break

3 Compliment Your Mirror Day

4 Independence Day

5 Workaholics Day

9 Special Recreation Day

15 Respect Canada Day

16 National Ice Cream Day

24 Pioneer Day—anniversary of the day Brigham Young reached the Salt Lake Valley (1847)

27 Take Your House Plant for a Walk Day

30 Comedy Celebration Day

31 First U.S. Patent Grant signed (1790)

Celebrations for the Month of August

Monthly Celebrations

Foot Health Month
National Catfish Month
National Water Quality Month

Weekly Celebrations

International Clown Week (1st week)
Beauty Queen Week
Don't Wait: Celebrate! Week—celebrate small but significant accomplishments (2nd week)
All American Soap Box Derby (2nd week)
National Smile Week (2nd week)
Elvis Week (3rd week)
Columbus Days (3rd week)
National Hosiery Week (3rd week)
Bald Eagle Days (3rd week)
Be Kind to Humankind Week (Final week)

Daily Celebrations

1st Sunday	American Family Day
1	Anniversary of the last entry of the diary of Anne Frank
1	Sports Day—promoting sportsmanship in the United States in all fields, from business to politics, race relations to sports
4	Bratwurst Days (4th–5th)
4	Coast Guard Day (since 1970)
5	National Mustard Day
5	Celebration of Peace Day
6	Friendship Day
6	Hiroshima Day—First atomic bomb dropped on Hiroshima from a B-29 Superfortress (1945)
9	Resignation Day—Richard M. Nixon resigns (1974)
11	Presidential Joke Day
12	Old-Time Farm Day
12	Civil War Days (12th–13th)
13	Birthday of American markswoman Annie Oakley (1860–1926)

14 Liberty Tree Day

15 National Relaxation Day

17 Birthday of David Crockett (1786–1836)

18 Bad Poetry Day

19 National Aviation Day

20 National Homeless Animals Day

22 Be an Angel Day—perform one small act of service for someone

23 Birthday of actor/dancer Gene Kelly (1912–1996)

25 Kiss and Make Up Day

26 Make Your Own Luck Day

26 Women's Equality Day

28 First radio commercial airs (1922)

29 More Herbs, Less Salt Day

Celebrations for the Month of September

Monthly Celebrations

National Hispanic Heritage Month
Healthy Aging Month
Women of Achievement Month
Self-Improvement Month
Southern Gospel Music Month
National Rice Month
National Piano Month
National Papaya Month
National Honey Month
National Courtesy Month
National Chicken Month

Weekly Celebration

National Rub a Bald Head Week (2nd week)
Fall Hat Week (2nd week)
National Adult Day Care Week (3rd week)
Religious Freedom Week (Final week)
National Dog Week (Final week)

Daily Celebrations

Rosh Hashanah (Jewish New Year) usually occurs in September

1st Sunday	National Grandparents Day
1st Monday	Labor Day (observed)
4th Sunday	National Good Neighbor Day
4th Friday	American Indian Day
2	V-J Day—celebrating the end of fighting in WWII (1945)
2	Box Car Days
5	Be Late for Something Day
6	National Do It Day or Fight Procrastination Day
7	Grandma Moses Day
10	Swap Ideas Day
11	Patriot Day
13	Birthday of actress Claudette Colbert (1905–1996)

13   Anniversary of the inspiration for the Star-Spangled Banner (1814)

14   International Cross-Culture Day

14   National Anthem Day

15   Respect for the Aged Day in Japan

17   Wool Day

17   National Constitution Day

17   Citizenship Day

18   U.S. Air Force established (1947)

19   International Day of Peace

21   World Gratitude Day

22   Ice Cream Cone invented (1903)

23   Pancake Day

24   Kids' Day

24   National Bluebird of Happiness Day

24   Birthday of F. Scott Fitzgerald (1896–1940)

24   Anniversary of the death of Theodore Geisel (Dr. Seuss; 1904-1991)

25   Pacific Ocean Day—Vasco Nunez de Balboa discovers the Pacific Ocean (1513)

26   Birthday of Johnny Appleseed (1774–1845)

27   Ancestor Appreciation Day

28   First night football game held in Mansfield, PA (1892)

30   Babe Ruth's Last Game as a Yankee (1934)

Celebrations for the Month of October

Monthly Celebrations

National Apple Jack Month
Country Music Month
National Popcorn Month
National Pretzel Month
Family History Month
National Dessert Month
National Pasta Month
National Pizza Month
Polish American Heritage Month

Weekly Celebrations

National Spinning and Weaving Week (1st week)
National Pickled Pepper Week (2nd week)
National Pet Peeve Week (2nd week)
National Fire Prevention Week (2nd week)
International Letter Writing Week (2nd week)
National Newspaper Week (2nd week)
Peace With Justice Week (3rd week)
National Sunshine Week (3rd week)
National Magic Week (Final week)
Peace, Friendship, and Good Will Week (Final week)

Daily Celebrations

Yom Kippur usually occurs in October

2nd Monday   Columbus Day

3rd Saturday   Sweetest Day

1   World Vegetarian Day

1   U.S. Agricultural Fair Day—anniversary of the first agricultural fair in the United States at Pittsfield, Massachusetts (1810)

2   Name Your Car Day—Honor your car by giving it a name

2   World Farm Animal Day

3   *The Andy Griffith Show* debuts (1960)

4   Sputnik I, the first artificial satellite, launched into orbit by the Russians (1957)

4   Yom Kippur or Day of Attonement—Jewish holiday

6   National German-American Day—celebration of German heritage

8   *The Adventures of Ozzie and Harriet* debuts on radio (1944)

9   Native American Day

11   Birthday of Eleanor Roosevelt (1928–1993)

12   National Dessert Day

14   Annual Be Bald and Be Free Day

15   National Grouch Day

15   World Poetry Day

16   World Food Day

17   Black Poetry Day

22   Mother-in-Law Day

23   TV Talk Show Host Day

24   United Nations Day

26   Red Cross/Red Crescent formed (1863)

27   Navy Day

28   St. Jude's Day

29   Anniversary of the disastrous stock market crash (1929) that was the starting point of the Great Depression

31   National Magic Day—anniversary of the death of Harry Houdini (1874–1926)

31   Halloween

Celebrations for the Month of November

Monthly Celebrations

National Ice Skating Month
National Jewish Book Month
One Nation Under God Month
Home and Family Month
National Stamp Collecting Month
Peanut Butter Lover's Month
Real Jewelry Month

Weekly Celebrations

National Family Caregivers Week
National Fig Week (1st week)
World Communication Week (1st week)
National Split Pea Soup Week (2nd week)
National Geography Awareness Week (3rd week)
National Children's Book Week (3rd week)
National Adoption Week (week of Thanksgiving)
National Bible Week (Sunday before Thanksgiving to the following Sunday)
National Game and Puzzle Week (Final week)

Daily Celebrations

1st Tuesday after 1st Monday Election Day
3rd Thursday Great American Smokeout
4th Thursday Thanksgiving
Sunday before Thanksgiving National Bible Sunday

1 All Saints Day/All Hallows Day—Roman Catholic Holy Day
1 National Author's Day
2 All Souls Day
2 Birthday of Daniel Boone (1734–1845)
3 Sandwich Day
5 Birthday of Will Rogers (1879–1935)
6 Saxophone Day (1814)
8 Birthday of actress Katherine Hepburn (1907–)
8 X-ray Discovery Day (1895)
11 Veterans' Day

14 Birthday of Robert Fulton (1965–1815)

15 American Enterprise Day—celebrate the achievements of America's free market economy

15 National Clean Out Your Refrigerator Day

17 Homemade Bread Day

19 Have a Bad Day Day

21 World Hello Day

23 Birthday of Harpo Marx (1893–1964)

23 Birthday of Billy the Kid (1859–1881)

26 *Casablanca* released (1942)

29 Birthday of Louisa May Alcott, author of *Little Women* (1832–1888)

30 Stay Home Because You're Well Day

Celebrations for the Month of December

Monthly Celebration

Modern Bingo's Birthday Month
National Stress-Free Month
Universal Human Rights Month

Weekly Celebrations

Human Rights Week (2nd week)

Daily Celebrations

Hanukkah generally occurs in December, but may begin in late November

2   Monroe Doctrine Day

2   Plan American Health Day

3   Heart Transplant Day—anniversary of the first human heart transplant (1967)

5   Birthday of Walt Disney (1901–1966)

6   St. Nicholas' Day—day to retell the legends of St. Nicholas

7   Pearl Harbor Day (1941)

8   Beach Day or Blessing of the Water Day

8   Mother's Day in Spain

8   Feast of Immaculate Conception—Roman Catholic Holy Day

10   Human Rights Day

11   Most Boring Celebrities of the Year Day

12   Poinsettia Day

12   Pennsylvania Admission Day—Pennsylvania entered the Union as the 2nd of the 13 original states (1787)

13   Noel Night

14   South Pole discovered (1911)

15   Underdog Day

15   Bill of Rights Day

16   Boston Tea Party Anniversary

16   Eat What You Want Day

17   Aviation Day—Wright Brothers' first flight, Kitty Hawk, North Carolina (1903)

20   Louisiana Purchase Day

21   Forefathers' Day—landing at the Plymouth Rock (1620)

21   First day of winter/Winter solstice

22   International Arbor Day

23   First flight around the world without refueling lands (1986)

24   Christmas Eve

25   Christmas Day

26   First day of Kwanzaa—a celebration of African heritage

27   Radio City Music Hall opens (1932)

29   Most Dubious News Stories of the Year Day

31   New Year's Eve

Appendix B

101 Things to Do With the Person Who Has Alzheimer's Disease

101 Things To Do With the Person Who Has Alzheimer's Disease

1. Clip coupons

2. Sort poker chips

3. Count tickets

4. Rake leaves

5. Use the carpet sweeper

6. Read aloud

7. Bake cookies

8. Look up names in the phone book

9. Read the daily newspaper aloud

10. Ask someone who has a baby or young child to visit

11. Listen to polka music

12. Plant seeds indoors or outdoors

13. Look at family photographs

14. Toss a ball

15. Color pictures

16. Make homemade lemonade

17. Wipe off the table

18. Weed the flower bed

19. Make cream cheese mints

20. Have a spelling bee

21. Read the *Reader's Digest* aloud

22. Fold clothes

23. Have a calm pet visit

24. Cut pictures out of greeting cards

25. Wash silverware

26. Bake homemade bread

27. Sort objects such as beads by shape or color

28. Sing Christmas carols

29. Say "tell me more" when they start talking about a memory

30. Put silverware away

31. Make a Valentine collage

32. Play favorite songs and sing together

33. Take a ride

34. Make a cherry pie

35. Read aloud from labels

36. Dye Easter eggs

37. Make a basket of socks

38. Take a walk

39. Reminisce about the first day of school

40. String Cheerios to hang outside for the birds

41. Make a fresh fruit salad

42. Sweep the patio

43. Color paper shamrocks green

44. Fold towels

45. Have afternoon tea

46. Remember great inventions

47. Play Pictionary

48. Paint a sheet

49. Cut out paper dolls

50. Identify states and capitols

51. Make a family tree poster

52. Color a picture of our flag

53. Cook hot dogs outside

54. Grow magic rocks

55. Water house plants

56. Reminisce about their first kiss

57. Play horseshoes

58. Dance

59. Sing favorite hymns

60. Make homemade ice cream

61. Force bulbs for winter blooming

62. Make Christmas cards

63. Sort playing cards by their color

64. Write a letter to a family member

65. Dress in red on a football Saturday

66. Pop popcorn

67. Name the Presidents

68. Give a manicure

69. Make paper butterflies

70. Plant a tree

71. Make a May basket

72. Make homemade applesauce

73. Finish famous sayings

74. Feed ducks

75. Mold with Play Doh

76. Look at pictures in *National Geographic*

77. Put together a simple puzzle

78. Sand wood

79. Rub in hand lotion with a pleasant scent

80. Decorate paper place mats

81. Arrange fresh flowers

82. Remember famous people

83. Straighten underwear drawers

84. Finish nursery rhymes

85. Make peanut butter sandwiches

86. Wipe off patio furniture

87. Cut up used paper for scratch paper

88. Take care of a fish tank

89. Trace and cut out leaves

90. Ask simple questions

91. Finish Bible quotes

92. Paint with string

93. Cut out pictures from magazines

94. Read classic short stories

95. Put coins into a jar

96. Sew sewing cards

97. Put bird feed out for birds

98. Clean out a pumpkin

99. Reminisce about a favorite summer

100. Roll yarn into a ball

101. Make a birthday cake

Appendix C

The Importance of
Good Communication Skills

The Importance of Good Communication Skills

Prepared at Eastern Michigan University in collaboration with the Alzheimer's Association–Greater Ann Arbor chapter with a grant from the Department of Mental Health. Written by Anne Robinson, Beth Spencer, and Laurie White. Copyright September 1988. This material may be duplicated with proper acknowledgment.

Communicating with a person with a dementing illness such as Alzheimer's disease can be a terribly difficult task. Often in early stages of a dementing illness people have trouble finding the words to express their thoughts or may be unable to remember the meaning of simple words or phrases. These problems, however, are usually minor inconveniences or frustrations. The later stages may be more difficult with language skills quite impaired, resulting in nonsensical, garbled statements and great difficulty in understanding.

When people cannot comprehend what is being said or cannot find the words to express their own thoughts, it can be painful, frustrating, and embarrassing for everyone. The following are some suggestions of things to think about when communicating with an impaired person.

Your Approach: You Set the Tone

Think about how you are presenting yourself. Are you tense? frowning? being bossy or controlling? People with dementia are often extremely aware of nonverbal signals, such as facial expression, body tension, and mood. If you are angry or tense, they are likely to become angry, anxious, or annoyed.

Try a calm, gentle, matter-of-fact approach. You set the mood for interaction—your relaxed manner may be contagious.

Use a nondemanding approach—try humor, cajoling, cheerfulness. Humor or gentle teasing often helps caregivers through difficult moments. Convincing someone to get out of bed or to the bathroom is usually easier if you can make a game or joke or it. Ordering or demanding may be much less successful with some people.

Try using touch to help convey your message. Sometimes touch can show that you care, even when your words don't or when you are not understood. Some people shy away from being touched, but most find a gentle touch reassuring.

Begin your conversation socially. Winning the person's trust first can often make a task much simpler. One way of doing this is to spend some time chatting before approaching the task at hand. For example, you might spend ten minutes talking about the weather, or family members, or some reassuring topic, to get the person in a relaxed frame of mind. Again, you are creating a pleasant mood.

Things to Think About When You Speak

Talk to the person in a place free from distractions such as equipment noise, television, or other conversations. People with dementia often have very little ability to screen out distractions.

Begin conversations with orienting information. Identify yourself if necessary and call the person by name. After creating a relaxed atmosphere, explain what you propose to do.

Look directly at the person and make sure you have his or her attention before you begin to speak. If you cannot get the person's attention, wait a few minutes and try again. Move slowly. Gently touch an arm or hand to gain attention while saying the person's name several times. Be careful not to startle him or her.

Be at eye level with the person, especially when talking to people who are very impaired or hard of hearing.

Speak slowly and say individual words clearly. This is particularly important for people with hearing problems or those in the later stages of dementia.

Use short, simple sentences. People with dementia may not be able to remember more than a few words at a time. Pause between sentences and allow plenty of time for the information to be understood.

Ask questions that require a simple choice or a yes or no answer rather than open-ended questions. For example, instead of saying "What would you like to wear today?" say "Do you want to wear the green dress or the red one?" or "Is this the dress you would like to wear today?"

Use concrete terms and familiar words. As people become more impaired they lose the ability to understand abstract concepts. Thus you may need to say, "Here is your soup at this table" rather than "It's time for lunch." They may also revert to words from childhood or earlier in life, so that "Do you need to use the bathroom?" may not be understood as easily as "Do you have to pee?"

Speak in a warm, easygoing, pleasant manner. Try to use a tone of voice that you would like people to use with you.

Keep the pitch of your voice low. Sometimes when people don't immediately understand us, we have a tendency to shout. This will simply upset the person with dementia and will make communication more difficult.

When Doing a Task Together

Try to focus on familiar skills or tasks. People with dementing illnesses gradually lose the ability to learn new tasks, but may be able to do familiar work, hobby-related tasks, or household chores even when very impaired.

Give choices whenever possible. For example, choosing whether to take a bath before or after dinner or choosing which of two shirts to wear may help the person to continue to feel some sense of control over his or her life.

Allow plenty of time for the information to be absorbed. People with dementia often need much more time to absorb simple statements of instruction. Allow a moment of silence before gently repeating an instruction. This requires a lot of patience on the part of caregivers.

Repeat instructions exactly the same way. It may take a number of repetitions before the person responds. If after allowing plenty of time it is still not understood, try using different key words or demonstrating what you want the person to do.

Break down the task into simple steps. Most of our daily tasks are very complex activities. The concepts of "getting dressed" or "taking a bath" may be too overwhelming and abstract for a person with a dementing illness. The person may be able to respond better to smaller, concrete steps—one part of the task at a time. For example, the first step in getting dressed might be unbuttoning pajamas. The second step might be taking the right arm out of the sleeve, and so forth. Find out which steps the person is able to do and encourage those. Gently help with the most difficult steps. Although this technique takes time and practice, doing tasks together can become much more successful and pleasant.

Modify the steps as the person becomes more impaired. You may need to break tasks into even smaller steps or you may need to gently begin doing some of the steps that the person was able to do previously. Again, this takes time and patience on the part of the caregiver, but it can be very rewarding for both the person with dementia and the caregiver.

Praise sincerely for success. We all need to hear that we are doing a good job. For people losing their abilities, it may be particularly important. Praise doesn't need to be long or gushy—it may be a simple "thank you" or "you did a nice job."

When You Are Having Trouble Being Understood

Listen actively and carefully to what the person is trying to say. If you do not understand, apologize and ask the person to repeat it. Let him or her know when you do understand by repeating it or rephrasing it.

Try to focus on a word or phrase that makes sense. Repeat that back to the person to help him or her clarify what is being said.

Respond to the emotional tone of the statement. You may not understand what is being said but you may recognize that it is being said angrily or sadly. Saying "you sound very angry" at least acknowledges the feelings, even if you cannot decipher the words.

Try to stay calm and to be patient. Remember the person is not doing this on purpose and is probably even more frustrated than you. Your calmness and patience will create a caring atmosphere that will encourage the person to keep trying.

Ask family members about possible meanings for words, names, or phrases you do not understand. Sometimes people with dementia talk in a kind of code that may make sense to people who have known them for a long time. A name called over and over may be a close friend or relative from the past whose memory is reassuring. "Let's go down that street to my house" may be a very logical way of referring to a long corridor and room, when names for those places have disappeared from memory. Language from childhood, such as names for bathroom habits or pet names for things, may reappear in the person's vocabulary. While it is helpful to use such words (e.g., "pee" or "tinkle"), it is important to continue to treat people as adults, not children.

Things NOT To Do

Don't argue with the person. This always makes the situation worse. Remember that a person with dementia no longer has the ability to be rational or logical to the extent you do.

Don't order the person around. Few of us like to be bossed around and the person with dementia is no exception. Even when your words are not understood, your tone of voice will be.

Don't tell the person what he or she can't do. State directions positively instead of negatively. Instead of "You can't go outside now" try "Let's sit down here and look at these pictures."

Don't be condescending. It is hard not to use a condescending tone of voice when you are speaking slowly and in short sentences; however, a condescending tone is likely to provoke anger, even if the words are not understood.

Don't ask a lot of direct questions that rely on a good memory. Often our attempts at being sociable involve asking people about themselves. Remember that people with dementia have memory loss and may feel humiliated or angry if you ask questions they can no longer answer. For example, instead of asking, "Who is this in the picture?" say, "The woman in this photo is lovely." Then the participant could either graciously agree (if he or she does not recognize the woman) or offer more information if known ("Yes, that's my daughter, Jane.")

Don't talk about people in front of them. It is easy to fall into the habit of talking about people in front of them when they can no longer communicate well. It is impossible to know how much someone with dementia understands, and this may vary from moment to moment.

When Verbal Communication Fails

Try distracting the person. Sometimes simply diverting the person's attention to other activities—going for a walk, changing the subject, offering a snack, or turning on the television—may be enough to diffuse an angry or anxious mood. Try again later.

Ignore a verbal outburst if you can't think of any positive response. It is much better to ignore angry or agitated statements than to become angry yourself. You might also try apologizing and letting the subject drop, or changing the emotional tone of the conversation (e.g., making a positive, cheerful comment instead of an angry reply).

Try other forms of communicating. Many ways of communicating don't involve words. Familiar songs, gentle touching or massage, favorite foods, or walking together can often demonstrate concern and affection more effectively than words. These modes of communicating can also help to soothe a troubled person and take the edge off difficult moments.

Suggested Resources

Allen, Jr., S. *Rx for health through creative silliness—Juggling life's stress.* [Videotape]. Author.

Anisman-Saltman, J. (1989). *Laughter: Rx for survival* [Videotape]. Cheshire, CT: Creative Awareness Center.

Beisgen, B.A. (1989). *Life-enhancing activities for mentally impaired elders.* New York, NY: Springer Publishing Company.

Breske, S. (1994, March). Jest for the Health of It. *Advance/Rehabilitation.*

Carlson, D.M. and Foster, B.G. (2000). *Reaching communities with Alzheimer's education: A comprehensive, advanced train-the-trainer manual* (2nd ed.). Reno, NV: Eymann Publications, Inc.

Cousins, N. (1979). *Anatomy of an illness.* New York, NY: Norton Publishing.

Dezan, N. (1994). *Barbers, cars, and cigars: Activity programming for older men.* Mt. Airy, MD: Eldersong Publishing.

Goodwin, D. (1986). *The activity director's bag of tricks* (Rev. ed.). Snellville, GA: The Activity Factory.

Helgeson, E.M. and Willis, S.C. (1987). *Handbook of group activities for impaired older adults.* Binghamton, NY: The Haworth Press.

Lally, S. (1991, August 28). Stress? Laugh it off. *The Washington Post.*

Mace, N.L. and Rabins, P.V. (1999). *The 36-hour day: A family guide to caring for persons with Alheimer disease, related dementing illnesses, and memory loss in later life* (3rd ed.). Baltimore, MD: Johns Hopkins University Press.

McGowin, D.F. (1993). *Living in the labyrinth: A personal journey through the maze of Alzheimer's.* Forest Knolls, CA: Elder Books.

Morreall, J. (1982). *Taking laughter seriously.* Albany, NY: SUNY Press.

Nahemow, L., McCluskey-Fawcett, K.A., and McGhee, P.E. (Eds). (1986). *Humor and aging.* Orlando, FL: Academic Press, Inc.

Parker, S.D., Will, C., and Burke, C.L. (1989). *Activities for the elderly.* Baltimore, MD: National Health Publishing.

Peterson, K. (1991, March 29). The HUMOR project fights stressful world. *The Daily Gazette.*

Thews, V., Reaves, A.M., and Henry, R.S. (Eds.). (1993). *Now what? A handbook of activities for adult day programs.* Winston-Salem, NC: Bowman Gray School of Medicine of Wake Forest University.

Zgola, J.M. (1987). *Doing things: A guide to programming activities for persons with Alzheimer's disease and related disorders.* Baltimore, MD: Johns Hopkins University Press.

Activity-Related Catalogs

Activity Director's Catalog
Sea Bay Game Company
77 Cliffwood Avenue, Suite 1D, Cliffwood, NJ 07721
Phone (800) 568-0188; Fax (732) 583-7284
http://www.seabaygame.com
Variety of games, tapes, instruments, supplies, and books

Briggs Activity and Recreation Products
Briggs Corporation
P.O. Box 1698, Des Moines, IA 50309–1698
Phone (877) 307-1744; Fax (800) 222-1996
http://www.briggscorp.com
Activity products, forms, tapes, medical supplies, and charting equipment

S & S Products for Healthcare
S & S Worldwide
P.O. Box 513, 75 Mill Street, Colchester, CT 06415
Phone (800) 243-9232; Fax (800) 547-6678
http://www.snswide.com
Art and craft supplies good for diagnostic, rehabilitative, and educational situations, as well as adaptive aids for crafts

Sammons, Source for ADL Products
Sammons Preston, Inc.
4 Sammons Court, Bolingbrook, IL 60440
Phone (800) 323-5547; Fax (800) 547-4333
Supplies, accessories, mobility, communication, assessment programs, treatment accessories, clinic equipment, exercise, and work therapy

World Wide Games Catalog
World Wide Games Corporation
P.O. Box 517, Colchester, CT 06415
Phone (800) 243-9232
Quality action games for recreation, therapy, and education

Organization

The HUMOR Project, Inc.
480 Broadway Suite 210
Saratoga Springs, NY 12866
Phone: (518) 587-8770
http://www.humorproject.com
The mission of The Humor Project, Inc. is to make a positive difference in the
lives of individuals and organizations through the use of publications, videos,
software, a mail-order catalog, and other humor resources.

Final Thoughts

In writing this manual, we had the opportunity to speak with many activity directors and related professionals. They shared ideas with us, expressed their opinions, and confided their problems and frustrations. We thank them for their assistance and candor.

One realization that came out of these discussions was that there needs to be more networking among people in the activities field. Manuals have their place—at least we certainly hope so! We chose to adopt a conversational tone to convey the feeling that we were exchanging ideas with our peers, rather than lecturing from a position of authority.

However, no manual can take the place of a face-to-face conversation with those who share similar concerns. Activity directors sometimes feel isolated from other staff members, such as medical personnel and administrators. Their responsibilities are unique, and only another activity person can truly understand the challenges they face.

Our final suggestion is that you look for ways to interact with others in the field of gerontological activities. Whether you form an official organization or just meet for coffee once in a while, you will undoubtedly find your best ideas and supports from others who have already walked many miles in your shoes.

Activity Index

G

Games

Gardening

Geography

Golf

H

Hanukkah

Holidays

Humor Activities

I

Independence Day

Intergenerational Activities

International

K

King, Martin Luther

Kite

Other Books by Venture Publishing, Inc.

The A•B•Cs of Behavior Change: Skills for Working With Behavior Problems in Nursing Homes
by Margaret D. Cohn, Michael A. Smyer, and Ann L. Horgas

Activity Experiences and Programming within Long-Term Care
by Ted Tedrick and Elaine R. Green

The Activity Gourmet
by Peggy Powers

Advanced Concepts for Geriatric Nursing Assistants
by Carolyn A. McDonald

Adventure Programming
edited by John C. Miles and Simon Priest

Assessment: The Cornerstone of Activity Programs
by Ruth Perschbacher

Behavior Modification in Therapeutic Recreation: An Introductory Manual
by John Datillo and William D. Murphy

Benefits of Leisure
edited by B. L. Driver, Perry J. Brown, and George L. Peterson

Benefits of Recreation Research Update
by Judy M. Sefton and W. Kerry Mummery

Beyond Bingo: Innovative Programs for the New Senior
by Sal Arrigo, Jr., Ann Lewis, and Hank Mattimore

Beyond Bingo 2: More Innovative Programs for the New Senior
by Sal Arrigo, Jr.

Both Gains and Gaps: Feminist Perspectives on Women's Leisure
by Karla Henderson, M. Deborah Bialeschki, Susan M. Shaw, and Valeria J. Freysinger

Client Assessment in Therapeutic Recreation Services
by Norma J. Stumbo

Conceptual Foundations for Therapeutic Recreation
edited by David R. Austin, John Datillo, and Bryan P. McCormick

Dimensions of Choice: A Qualitative Approach to Recreation, Parks, and Leisure Research
by Karla A. Henderson

Dementia Care Programming: An Identity-Focused Approach
By Rosemary Dunne

Diversity and the Recreation Profession: Organizational Perspectives
edited by Maria T. Allison and Ingrid E. Schneider

Effective Management in Therapeutic Recreation Service
by Gerald S. O'Morrow and Marcia Jean Carter

Evaluating Leisure Services: Making Enlightened Decisions, Second Edition
by Karla A. Henderson and M. Deborah Bialeschki

Everything From A to Y: The Zest Is up to You! Older Adult Activities for Every Day of the Year
by Nancy R. Cheshire and Martha L. Kenney

The Evolution of Leisure: Historical and Philosophical Perspectives
by Thomas Goodale and Geoffrey Godbey

Experience Marketing: Strategies for the New Millennium
by Ellen L. O'Sullivan and Kathy J. Spangler

Facilitation Techniques in Therapeutic Recreation
by John Datillo

File o' Fun: A Recreation Planner for Games & Activities, Third Edition
by Jane Harris Ericson and Diane Ruth Albright

The Game and Play Leader's Handbook: Facilitating Fun and Positive Interaction
by Bill Michaelis and John M. O'Connell

The Game Finder—A Leader's Guide to Great Activities
by Annette C. Moore

Getting People Involved in Life and Activities: Effective Motivating Techniques
by Jeanne Adams

Glossary of Recreation Therapy and Occupational Therapy
by David R. Austin

Great Special Events and Activities
by Annie Morton, Angie Prosser, and Sue Spangler

Venture Publishing, Inc.
1999 Cato Avenue
State College, PA 16801
Phone: (814) 234-4561
Fax: (814) 234-1651